P9-AQT-505

Images of War

The Vietnam Experience

Images of War

by Julene Fischer
and the picture staff of Boston Publishing Company

Text by Robert Stone

Boston Publishing Company/Boston, MA

WITHDRAWN

Jefferson-Madison
Regional Library
Charlottesville, Virginia

959.704
Fischer
(3)

Boston Publishing Company

President and Publisher: Robert J. George
Vice President: Richard S. Perkins, Jr.
Editor-in-Chief: Robert Manning
Managing Editor: Paul Dreyfus
Marketing Director: Jeanne Gibson

Senior Picture Editor: Julene Fischer
Senior Writers:
   Clark Dougan, Edward Doyle, David
   Fulghum, Samuel Lipsman, Terrence
   Maitland, Stephen Weiss
Senior Editor: Gordon Hardy

Picture Editors:
   Wendy Johnson, Lanng Tamura
Assistant Picture Editor: Kathleen A. Reidy

Picture Researchers:
   Nancy Katz Colman, Robert Ebbs,
   Tracey Rogers, Nana Elisabeth Stern,
   Shirley L. Green (Washington, D.C.),
   Kate Lewin (Paris)
Archivist: Kathryn J. Steeves
Picture Department Assistant:
   Karen Bjelke

Researchers:
   Richard J. Burke, Jonathan Elwitt,
   Sandra M. Jacobs, Steven W. Lipari, Michael Ludwig, Anthony Maybury-Lewis,
   Nicholas Philipson, Carole Rulnick, Ni-
   cole van Ackere, Janice Sue Wang, Robert Yarbrough

Production Editor: Kerstin Gorham
Assistant Production Editor:
Patricia Leal Welch
Assistant Editor: Denis Kennedy
Editorial Production:
   Sarah Burns, Theresa M. Slomkowski

Design: Designworks, Sally Bindari
Design Assistant: Emily Betsch

Business Staff:
Amy Pelletier, Amy P. Wilson

About the editors and authors:

Editor-in-Chief *Robert Manning*, a long-time journalist, has previously been editor-in-chief of the *Atlantic Monthly* magazine and its press. He served as assistant secretary of state for public affairs under Presidents John F. Kennedy and Lyndon B. Johnson. He has also been a fellow at the Institute of Politics at the John F. Kennedy School of Government at Harvard University.

Julene Fischer, senior picture editor at Boston Publishing Company, has headed the picture effort for THE VIETNAM EXPERIENCE since just after the beginning of the project. A graduate of the University of Colorado, she received her M.A. in English from the University of Washington.

Robert Stone covered Vietnam in 1971 for the British publications *Ink* and Manchester *Guardian*. His National Book Award-winning novel, *Dog Soldiers* (1974), grew out of his experiences there. In addition to writing for *LIFE*, *Harper's*, the *Atlantic Monthly*, and other periodicals, he has published three other novels, *Hall of Mirrors* (1967), *A Flag for Sunrise* (1981), and *Children of Light* (1986).

Picture Consultant: *Ngo Vinh Long* is a social historian specializing in China and Vietnam. Born in Vietnam, he returned there most recently in 1980.

Cover Photo:
Navy corpsman Vernon Wike tries vainly to save the life of a wounded Marine under fire during the battle of Hill 881 North, near Khe Sanh, spring 1967.

Copyright © 1986 by Sammler Kabinett Inc. All rights reserved. No part of this publication may be reproduced or transmitted in any form or by any means, electronic or mechanical, including photocopy, recording, or any information storage and retrieval system, without permission in writing from the publisher.

Library of Congress Catalog Card Number: 85-063001

ISBN: 0-939526-18-2

10 9 8 7 6
5 4 3 2

Contents

Preface

The Shattered Mirror

It was a war like no other. Americans are virtually unanimous about that, though they agree on few other certitudes about the war in Vietnam. Each earlier war left behind a widely accepted image or sense of its character. The Civil War was brother against brother. World War I was the war to end all wars. World War II was fought to stop Hitler's Nazism and Tojo's imperialism.

The image of the Vietnam War is a shattered mirror. In its shards, each onlooker finds his or her own private fragment of meaning or recollection.

What simple expression can, after the passage of little more than a decade, capture the essence or assess the meaning or the lessons learned from that bloody involvement thousands of miles from our shores—a war that contorted the national conscience and brought down the ruling political party? An enterprise born of noble ideals and impulses—yes, let us agree on that—but which, like some prehistoric monster lumbering blindly into the asphalt swamp, descended into tragedy? A venture that brought patriotism under fire at home, while summoning the best of patriotism among the many who fought in Vietnam—Americans and South and North Vietnamese?

Historians blessed with greater distance from the events will be the ones to search out such an essence. For now, it is challenge enough to assemble, with balance and sensitivity, the chronicle of those twenty or more years of turbulent history and the people caught up in its currents.

Part of that story is this volume of images, reflections glittering in the fragments of the broken mirror. The Vietnam War was the most thoroughly photographed combat in history. The camera's eye recorded it all—a GI sobbing over a dead buddy, a naked Vietnamese child fleeing a napalm attack, a Buddhist monk being consumed by flames, an American President brooding over events that have broken from his control, the joyous return of a hero from a Hanoi prison, the grisly sight of villagers slain by Vietcong guerrillas.

Words too have the power to evoke images. Such words as courage, sacrifice, brotherhood, tenacity, words that time and again found their application to men on both sides of the fighting. Or other words that buzz ominously in memory like insects. Body count. Pacification. Tonkin Gulf. Kent State. Boat people. "Hell, no! We won't go!" Pol Pot. The prison called Hanoi Hilton with its torture rooms. The bloodied highway ironically called the Street of Joy.

Some of the most vivid reflections of Vietnam came in the remarkable stream of books written by those who fought in or observed the war at close hand. One of those writers is Robert Stone, whose novel *Dog Soldiers* rates high among the books induced by the Vietnam War. He covered the combat in 1971. Mr. Stone was invited to write the text for this volume, adding his powerful word images to the portfolio of photographs selected by our picture editors and researchers. Together, they assemble many fragments of the shattered mirror in which Americans can try to view the war that was like no other.

—Robert Manning

Introduction

"There it is," they used to say in Vietnam. It was as if an evil spirit were loose, one of the demons known to the Vietnamese as *ma*, weaving in and out of visible reality, a dancing ghost. It would appear suddenly out of whirl, shimmer for an instant, and be lost. People came to recognize it. Recognizing it, they would say without excitement: "There it is," with emphasis on the last word to let their friends

On this page and the following three pages appear some of the war's most remembered images.

A medic at Chu Pong, 1966.

know that they had seen it and to be sure their friends had seen it too.

It was without form itself, but it could assume an infinity of forms. It was as tiny as a lizard's eye and as huge as the bad, black sky. It became events. It became things themselves.

It was at the heart of every irony, however innocuous, however hideously cruel. It might appear as a droll incongruity along some nameless road or as guilty laughter over things that weren't funny. It was as palpable as a tumbling bullet. It was lacy as light, fine enough to seep right into your deepest inward places and confront you as an oddly turned thought, a grotesque insight.

It had no strength of its own because it used human strength. It had no life of its own because it used human lives with a brave prodigality. Because it used so many young lives it could assume a youthful, frolicsome aspect. It could display its Alice in Wonderland side. There were comparisons to Alice in Wonderland. It was said that everything was

Through the Looking Glass and that there was Lewis Carroll logic. Red Queen to White Rabbit. There it is.

In fact, its Lewis Carroll dimension was moral. It had all the obsessiveness of Alice in Wonderland and about as much justice and mercy.

Some people called it the Gray Rat, This Shit, or The Show. Some called it Mr. Gray Rat. A Marine I knew called it Captain Gray Rat versus The World.

There exists a peculiar nomenclature. Among Union soldiers, the American Civil War was called The Elephant. Before Shiloh and Chancellorsville, some sergeant would inform the plowboys who had never been in the line before that they were Going to See the Elephant. That was what going into combat was called then.

The Marine mentioned above was on Operation Prairie around the Rockpile in 1967. In one fight during Operation Prairie, 32 Marines held off steady attacks by

Awaiting evacuation. Hue, 1968.

300 North Vietnamese Army regulars for two days. It was called the Groucho Marx Battle. My Marine friend said Operation Prairie was a Walt Disney True Life Adventure. He was badly wounded there, so badly that the first doctor who saw him decided to amputate his right hand but changed his mind at the last minute. The Marine's hand was saved and he was credited with a partial disability. He saw Captain Gray Rat versus The World as a Saturday morning cartoon in which you got killed.

Understand how young a lot of these people were. Their youth was a factor in how they thought and spoke. For example, they would not say things, they

Below. The crush to escape. Nha Trang, 1975. Bottom. Street execution. Saigon, 1968.

would go them. "So the gunny goes—'You been doggin' the bush, Smith?' So I go 'hell no, gunny!'" The average American infantryman in Vietnam was seven and a half years younger than his counterpart in the Second World War.

In those days it was unsettling to hear so much bitter whimsy from young Americans. Pre-Vietnam America had become a stranger to irony. These youths and their wit were brutally sophisticated. They'd all caught a glimpse of the *ma*, the war's infernal antic spirit.

"There it is!" they would say. There it was, the thing itself, but *what* was it? Whether they knew it or not, everyone was looking for a metaphor.

A napalmed tiger was a metaphor rich in implication. It was Captain Gray Rat's answer to culture shock, and The World's revenge on Nam, mysterious Asia beguiled. The colonial hunting preserves became free fire zones. Tigers prowling for corpses might find themselves incinerated on a hunch. Burning bright in the U Minh Forest, the tigers demonstrated the

bankruptcy of innocence. Nobody and nothing was innocent, or free, or neutral.

There was a metaphorical figure known as the Fool on the Hill, a figure of legend, compounded of fear and morning mist. The Fool might be hostile; bomb-proof, bulletproof, Luke the Gook. More dreadfully, he might be a duly authorized friendly sniper turned free-lance. Alone above a grapefruit patch, issued amphetamine to keep him alert, seduced by the relativity of things, the Fool might turn his fire anywhere. All motion was the same to him. He saw an essential gookishness deep down things, and he kept trying to kill it.

A hospital corpsman is running through a rice field carrying a small Vietnamese child. The child's been shot off the back of his water buffalo by the Fool on the Hill. Not content with shooting the child, the Fool has popped the buffalo as well. The corpsman runs with the bleeding child, making for dry ground, risking

On Mutter's Ridge. Operation Prairie, 1966.

submerged punji sticks and immersion foot. He knows the next thing the Fool will shoot may be him.

Eventually, if it were certain he was friendly, and if there were time, someone would have to go talk to the Fool and get him down and try to make him well again.

Buffaloes enraged the Fool with their basically foolish appearance. But anyone—a bored door gunner, a senior officer on his way to an inspection—might have a shot at a buffalo. Buffaloes didn't seem innocent. They chased people and they hated grunts. It was stupid to be chased by a buffalo. The animals were a useful metaphor because the human dimension was so painful and so hard to think about.

"Vengeance on a dumb brute ... seems blasphemous." So the Quaker Starbuck in *Moby Dick* sought to reason with Captain Ahab.

A race against death. Operation Prairie, 1966.

"Talk not to me of blasphemy, man," Ahab replied, "I'd strike the sun if it insulted me." He wasn't doing it for an abstraction like victory or for the oil. He was a moralist in an immoral world and he was going to fix it.

It's not gratuitous that *Moby Dick* is the great American novel and Ahab, with his passion for control and his "can do" spirit, is an American hero. Ahab started out chasing the whale because it represented everything that was wrong with the world. By the end of his disastrous voyage, no one remembered where goodness resided and the whale and the whalers went down together in a victory for no one at all.

In Laos, we used Cobra gunships against elephants on the Ho Chi Minh Trail. Descending like gigantic insects, the Cobras achieved complete surprise. They achieved complete astonishment as the first elephant exploded.

Once a young man from Missouri, an earnest German-American farm boy, slow spoken, Catholic, and bespectacled,

pondered a moral dilemma. Reasoning carefully, he decided the Vietnam War was wrong. He talked to his dad and went to Canada. In Canada he began to think he might have taken an easy way out. He came back and took the draft and went as a medic.

He was sent to I Corps, a known conshy, looking out at it all with his honest weak blue eyes. When he told them he wouldn't carry a weapon, they made him carry everybody's weapon on the way home. They kept it up until the first ambush. When the point went down and called for a medic they waited to see if he would go, and he went. They found out he would always go. Everybody loved him because he was without a grain of meanness, he liked to talk about important

Below. Convoy of tears. Highway 1, 1975. Bottom. Kent State, 1970.

things, and he had so much heart. Time passed. When he was short, his time in country nearly elapsed, no move was made to keep him out of the line. Other people complained on his behalf; he said not a word.

At that time they were fighting for hills on the Laotian border in I Corps. People were confused. The American command declared that it was not a war of hills. On one hill, they lost fifty-six men, and a general explained that the "hill had no military value whatsoever." There seemed to be a contradiction.

In these worthless hills the enemy liked to hurt the point to bring the medic up. They wanted the medicine and they would kill the medic to get it.

The man from Missouri died in a fight twenty-four hours long. When they killed him he was out of morphine, out of almost everything. He was bringing the wounded men mints as placebos. He went back to The World in a folding box

and it no longer mattered what he believed.

Strange rumors circulated about coffins. It was said that drugs were being smuggled out to The World in them. People said "there it is." It sounded a little too right to be true, but eventually the CID arrested some individuals at Aberdeen, Maryland, and their accomplices at Bien Hoa. Millions of dollars' worth of the purest heroin was being flown in with the KIAs. It turned out to be true after all. Then it was said that the gang at Aberdeen had missed one, and an undertaker in some tank town opened his son's coffin and found a bag full of smack beside the remains. That part was just rumor.

"There it is," we said, in our great sweep for metaphors. We never determined quite what it was. No single image served.

It was us. It was them. It was the cunning of dice play. The smoke, the rain, death—the destroyer of worlds, and the girls in the boom-boom rooms.

It was a mistake 10,000 miles long,

spinning out of control. Its fiery wash burned people down and processed adolescents into bags of garbage, sucked a million people out of their skin, and turned them into their own flayed ghosts.

The images we carried away are its embers. We will never forget it.

Decades ago, the historian Ralph Roeder in his classic study, *The Man of the Renaissance*, treated with a war now almost 500 years old, the invasion of Italy by King Charles VIII of France.

"Swollen by the confluence of so many causes," Roeder wrote, "it advanced like some complex, blundering, uncontrollable force which absorbed its own authors, and which assumed more and more the featureless and irresistible likeness of fate."

Humping. Near the DMZ, 1966.

Napalm strike. Highway 1, 1972.

Resisting the French

Vietnam's resistance to the French commenced even before the latter had completed their conquest of Indochina in the second half of the nineteenth century. The situation of a small country struggling against an imperial power was one the Vietnamese understood profoundly. Having resisted China for centuries, they knew all the weaknesses of an empire at war and all the advantages accruing to the guerrilla.

Beyond the limited circle directly profiting by French authority, the desire to be rid of French rule was universal, embracing all social classes. But the strongest and most enduring faction of the independence movement was that controlled by the Communist party of Vietnam. This was due in great measure to the fact that the most influential and resourceful fighter for Vietnamese independence was also one of the founding fathers of the Comintern, the man known to his early collaborators by the nom de guerre Nguyen Ai Quoc and later to all the world as Ho Chi Minh.

During World War II, a weak Vichy regime governed Vietnam at the sufferance of Japan. Foreseeing an Allied victory, Ho consolidated the resistance. From jungle redoubts, his Vietminh used traditional guerrilla tactics effectively against the Japanese.

Eventually the American forces of China Command came to recognize the Vietminh as the authentic representative of the Allied war effort in Indochina. A close collaboration developed between American OSS operatives and Ho's guerrillas.

As the war turned against them, the Japanese seized direct control of Indochina only to surrender it in defeat to the Vietminh. After over 100 years of French rule, the whole of Vietnam had an indigenous government.

Ho Chi Minh counted on his cordial relationship with the United States to protect Vietnamese autonomy. American policy seemed to favor the Vietminh. The United States, predominant in the Asian theater of war, opposed the restoration of French rule.

At one point, beset by Chinese pressure in the north and the arrival of British troops determined to install the regrouping French, Ho requested that the United States take Vietnam under its temporary control. His request was declined, but at ceremonies in Hanoi proclaiming an independent Vietnam, Ho announced his Vietnamese Declaration of Independence based in large part on America's.

Supported by Britain, the French returned in force. Quite soon, their armies were engaged in the most bitter of France's colonial wars. Time after time, their carefully planned "encirclements" ended in frustration. The terrain was hellish. Sixty percent of the country was a jungle that suffocated conventional armies. Monsoons and the high canopy of trees made air support difficult a large part of the year.

The enemy was skillful and ruthless, avoiding engagement, then striking at isolated posts or in cities thought to be secure. It was a dirty war, fought under demoralizing conditions. By 1954, the French were fighting their last losing battle at Dien Bien Phu.

In the interim, America's mood had changed. Her wartime anticolonialist policy had come to seem naive and even treacherous. China had been "lost" and grave accusations exchanged that would paralyze the country's Asian policy for a generation. Some strategists professed to detect an American interest in any anti-Communist war. America must bear any burden, it was said, to preserve the free world her power had created. Her power was vast, a mighty force for good.

America's attention turned toward the sea-horse-shaped "Lesser Dragon" of Vietnam. She had forgotten that in 1945 an American intelligence officer had declared in his last report that the white man was "finished" in Southeast Asia. She had forgotten her fierce, indomitable wartime allies and their ruthless, single-minded rejection of foreign control.

France, free of its dirty war, watched with some cynicism as America began the process of involvement in Vietnam.

The advance guard of the American Presence appeared in Saigon, and many found Vietnam charming, with its flame trees, cafés, and lovely women. At the same time, a French scholar was writing of French soldiers' agony as their road came to an end at Dien Bien Phu. Place names along that road—Ban Me Thuot, Dak To, An Khe, Hue—would one day be familiar in remote American towns. The Frenchman's book was entitled, *Hell in a Very Small Place.*

Vietnamese nationalists are hauled off to jail under the watchful eye of a French guard in the fall of 1945.

On August 19, 1945, 1,000 Vietminh soldiers entered Hanoi to drum up support for Ho Chi Minh, who was to declare Vietnamese independence three weeks later. Here, thousands of Hanoi residents gather in front of the Opera House as their revolutionary standard is unfurled.

Above. Ho Chi Minh proclaims independence for Vietnam in Hanoi on September 2, 1945.

Below. Ho's lieutenant, Vo Nguyen Giap (with plaid tie), and Major A.L.A. Patti of the U.S. Office of Strategic Services (to his right) salute the flags of their two countries, August 26, 1945.

Right. Preparing for war with the resurgent French colonial force in late 1946, Vietminh soldiers dig trenches inside the former residence of the French governor-general in Hanoi.

Above. Officers' evening mess at a French post at Phu Lo in the Red River Delta, early 1951. Later that evening the Vietminh attacked the post.

Right. French reinforcements sent north from Saigon crowd the decks of an American-built landing craft in Ha Long Bay in January 1951.

Hit by napalm, a village along the Song Lang burns during a French attack on November 4, 1953. The use of napalm against suspected enemy targets aroused protest from the French public.

Left. Dien Bien Phu. A French legionnaire stands wearily in a trench during a respite from nearly constant shelling by Vietminh guerrillas in early 1954.

Above. Vietminh soldiers, armed with World War II–vintage Japanese arms, work their way toward French lines at Dien Bien Phu. The fall of the outpost on May 7, 1954, dealt the final blow to French hopes for a revived colony in Indochina.

Above. French commanders at Dien Bien Phu contemplate their options during the doomed defense of their outpost. From left are Major Maurice Guiraud, Major Andre Botella, Lieutenant Colonel Marcel Bigeard, Major Pierre Tourret, Colonel Pierre Langlais, and Lieutenant Colonel Hubert de Seguins-Pazzis.

Right. Hanoi, 1954. Sixty-eight years after the first French flag was raised over the city, the Tricolor is lowered at French headquarters.

Saigon

The building that symbolized Saigon to the literate world was the Continental Palace Hotel, its high-vaulted ceilings abloom with enormous, slowly rotating fans. The hotel and its terrace restaurant would be forever associated with Graham Greene's *The Quiet American*. In the spring of 1971, the terrace by day looked much as it had in Greene's time, but the city had changed a great deal.

The former National Theater at the north end of Lam Son Square had become the National Assembly. Its gilt was peeling, its gardens were ill tended, and the plaza before it was a car park centering on a new military memorial of singular repulsiveness.

Facing the Continental from across the square stood the Hotel Caravelle, a sleek American job in which Graham Greene wouldn't have been caught dead. From the rooftop bar of the Caravelle you could watch outgoing rounds from the batteries at Tan Son Nhut and, sometimes, the bursting of parachute flares seeking out sappers along the field perimeter.

At the Caravelle bar they didn't know an apéritif from an apricot. Customers were expected to get drunk and spend a lot of money doing it. The big drinks sometimes attracted Scandinavian reporters whose left-wing views and anti-war sentiments would bring them into conflict with the burly civilian hard hats who worked for Morrison & Knudson or other contractors.

Saigon as a city had never been rooted in anything more than expedience; its charms were gratuitous or purely in the mind's eye. Its principal buildings, with the exception of fin de siècle artifacts like the Gia Long Palace or the Town Hall, tended toward art deco curves of opaque glass that, at their best, sug-

gested illustrations on the old Normandie's breakfast menu. The only thing Parisian about it was the number and quality of its better restaurants, the decline of which it was customary to bemoan.

That year the best and most expensive restaurant in Saigon was the Guillaume Tell in Khanh Hoi near the Ben Nghe Canal. Ramuntcho's in the Eden Passage near Lam Son Square was favored by the foreign press. Givral's, the famous ice cream parlor on Tu Do Street (which *The Quiet American* knew as the rue Catinat), did business a few doors from a Dairy Queen that served water buffalo hamburgers. Along the river front, down streets faintly reminiscent of New Orleans, was a floating restaurant that served Vietnamese food beyond compare. A few hundred yards upriver was that blackened hulk of its late competitor, the legendary My Canh, blown up prior to the battle of Saigon in 1968.

All along Tu Do and the streets adjoining it were massage parlors and bars catering to GIs. The GIs were few by 1971; only those personnel with jobs in the capital were permitted downtown. "Skag bars" that sold heroin were off-limits and watched by the military police. Most of the joints stood nearly empty behind their protective antigrenade wire. Inside, heavily made-up Vietnamese bargirls played solitaire before rows of unoccupied stools.

Americans walking the streets of Saigon felt accusing eyes on them. The Vietnamese, soldiers and civilians alike, had always known the scorn in which their allies held them. Jostlings and minor traffic accidents involving Americans became the scene of near riots. Insults were shouted in the face of passing Caucasians. The mood in the capital was evi-

dence that Hanoi had scored a measure of success in its battle to erode the South's morale.

The malaise hanging over the city shocked some returning reporters. Street crime increased, partly because dislocations and ARVN casualties had created a multitude of orphans or half-orphans whose mothers were driven into prostitution or something like it. On every corner stolen U.S. property was for sale. PX cameras, GI uniforms, M16s.

The smart money was beginning to shift assets. The Phu Tho race track, which had been a field hospital for the NVA during Tet 1968, was a race track again and the horses, better fed than most of Saigon's poor, ran for heavy purses every day.

In the hours just before curfew, an element of the city never observed before drifted downtown from the inner districts. Transvestites, junkies, and hoodlums, all quite local, appeared on the sedate terrace of the Continental. Long-haired groups of juvenile delinquents waited for drunks in the darkness outside.

What sustained the spirits of Saigon's extensive demimonde was the continued presence of the Indian moneychangers. From tiny offices beyond metal doors in the buildings over the Eden Passage, they traded in currency, offering as much as 500 Vietnamese piasters to the dollar. One morning, it was said, there would be a portent of the beginning of the end. Saigon would awaken and the Indians would be gone.

Soldiers gather outside the Rose Bar on Saigon's Tu Do Street, where bars and prostitution proliferated after the Americans arrived.

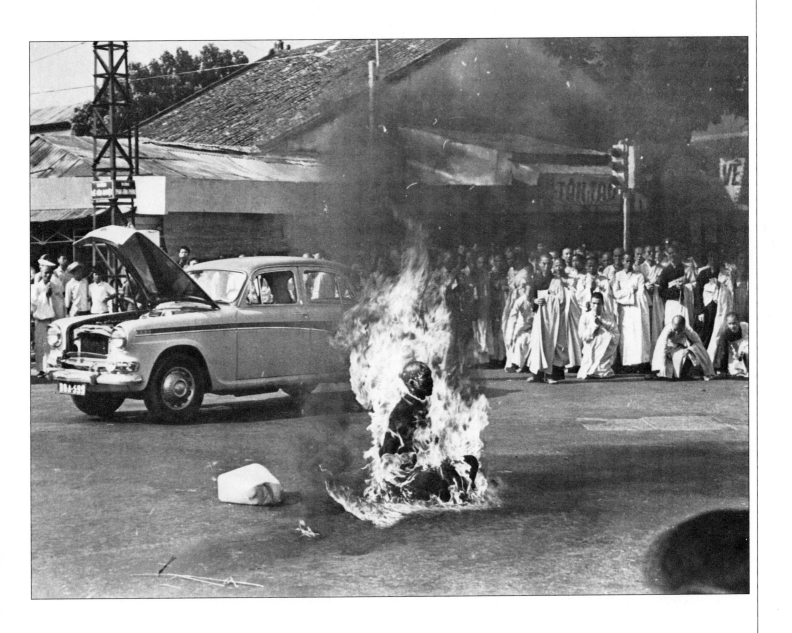

Left. South Vietnam's moody president, Ngo Dinh Diem, paces the floor of his Saigon palace after emerging victorious over the city's crime organization and armed sects who had attempted to oust him in the spring of 1955.

Above. An event that shocked the world. On June 11, 1963, the Buddhist monk Thich Quang Duc immolates himself on a Saigon boulevard to protest the anti-Buddhist policies of Diem, himself a Catholic. The waves of reaction to this and other Buddhist self-immolations further isolated Diem's increasingly unpopular regime.

The Diem regime falls. Madame Ngo Dinh
Nhu, Diem's sister-in-law, leaves her Bev-
erly Hills hotel after learning of the assassination of her husband and Diem on November 1, 1963. The president and his
brother, who had been Diem's right-hand
man, were slain after being ousted by a
group of disaffected generals.

New powers in Saigon. Lieutenant General
William C. Westmoreland confers with U.S.
Ambassador Henry Cabot Lodge in the
summer of 1964. American influence in
South Vietnam increased steadily after
Diem's death brought a succession of South
Vietnamese generals to power.

By the late 1960s, Saigon had become a garrison town, with large numbers of troops and a swelling refugee population. Here, a woman and child pass by barbwire on a city street in 1968.

Above. South Vietnam's Prime Minister Nguyen Cao Ky (left) and President Nguyen Van Thieu (right) confer with U.S. President Lyndon Johnson in Honolulu, February 1966. It was at this conference that LBJ committed the U.S. to increasing its efforts to pacify the South Vietnamese countryside.

Right. The body of a VC sapper lies inside the U.S. Embassy compound in Saigon, January 1968. During the Tet offensive, the spectacle of enemy troops penetrating an American sanctuary eroded confidence on both sides of the U.S.–South Vietnam alliance.

Left. The shacks of refugees choke Cholon, the Chinese district of Saigon, February 1969. By 1970, Saigon's population was 3 million; by 1972, its density of 70,000 residents per square mile exceeded that of Hong Kong, Tokyo, and New York.

Above. The influx of refugees from war-torn rural areas during the late 1960s caused unbearably crowded conditions in Saigon. Here, families have set up their homes in abandoned sewer pipes near the central market.

Left. A young Vietnamese peddles liquor from a black-market stand in Saigon. Much of the merchandise available in the thriving illegal markets was stolen from American military or economic aid shipments. For some, the black market was the principal means of survival in a city rife with official and unofficial corruption.

Above. A child, well-versed in the ways of street commerce, dickers with soldiers over souvenirs in a Saigon market, 1966. Standard practice for a buyer was to ask how much, offer half, then split the difference.

Above. Two American GIs tour the city in a pedicab in March 1966. The demand for services created by the presence of a foreign army intensified South Vietnam's economic dependence on the United States.

Right. An American construction worker strides past a beggar on Nguyen Thiep Street, Saigon, in 1970. Brought to South Vietnam to build the U.S. military infrastructure, civilians could enjoy a relatively luxurious standard of living.

A Saigon street erupts with protest against the corrupt Thieu regime during the 1971 elections. Government opposition escalated until 1975 and the Communist takeover.

War in the Village

In Saigon, toward the end of every work week, MACV would wonder about the villages. The villages were where the people were, and there was a theory current that the war would be lost or won among them.

MACV was a collective entity—Military Assistance Command, Vietnam—the organization in charge of the American military in Vietnam—but it had a name like a man's. I used to think of it as a man—a hairy-handed war chief out of the Celtic annals. Mac V of the Fiery Fist, Mac V of the Hundred Thousands.

One might picture Mac V of an evening, bending an ear toward the twilight forest, listening to whispers and murmurs. He was never certain what it was he heard.

In Washington they wanted everything on graphs. Mac V would have his wizards give them graphs. The graphs purported to reflect the allegiances of Vietnam's innumerable villages, the state of their hearts and minds. The graphs were on green printouts in black ink. Imagine Mac V, his broad brow furrowed, studying his copy of the graphs. His stout honest heart felt a queer foreboding, an unfamiliar sense of uncertainty. The printouts were called Hamlet Evaluation Reports.

The Asian village was a timeless social tool, an instrument of survival. It was a person's appointed place under heaven, his God-given place. Its ideal was harmony, continuity, peacefulness. Since the world was sometimes inharmonious, chaotic, and threatening, under pressure it could transform itself into a weapon. The village was the traditional weapon of the weak against the strong; half-hidden, resilient, yielding before pressure, then snapping back like a stake on a trip wire. Out of the village came such grim surprises as the tiger trap, the punji stick, the deadfall.

In theory, Mac V had crossed the ocean to help defend the villages of Vietnam but the theory was unsound. In many of the villages, an abiding love of the land and the children of the land, their countrymen, inclined the villagers' sympathies toward Mac V's enemies, the NLF guerrillas. The NLF surely was not above coercion; it excelled at coercion. But in contrast to the Americans, the NLF guerrillas were children of the land and therefore children of the people.

More often than not, young Americans entering the rural "villes" with their monosyllabic bebop names walked into a furnace of treachery and casually concealed hate. Exhausted, frightened, bereaved, the Americans stared into blank faces.

The Vietnamese villager never saw some reminder of his lost son or brother among what to him were crazy-looking oversized blond men or the crazy-looking oversized black ones. The Americans never got a sense of home from the frowning grannies or the frightened women whose unseeing eyes seemed to bid them despair and die. And though it might be thought that kids were the same everywhere, there were ugly stories about murderous children. Sophisticates on both sides smiled in mutual recognition. The villagers were seeing foreign devils. The Americans were seeing gooks.

The so-called Vietcong was turning out to be something very like the peasantry itself in arms.

In Malaya the British had used fortified villages defended by loyal inhabitants. Mac V employed the tactic in Vietnam although the circumstances were different. Thousands of peasants were removed from the soil of their ancestors, assembled, enclosed in wire. Mountain tribesmen and delta peasants were recruited as auxiliaries. Sustained efforts were made to separate friend from foe.

Mac V sighed. He was not without scruples. His trumpets gave forth an uncertain sound. Still, wars were to be won. Precautions had been taken and it was not time to talk of precautions any more. The other side destroyed its enemies in the villages without mercy. In World War II, the Allies had bombed the Dutch, the French, the Danes to get at Hitler. They had incinerated numberless Germans of every age and station. Mac V turned his fury on the villages.

Clouds of fire and steel descended on the countryside of Vietnam. It was demonstrated to recalcitrant peasants that their esteemed townships were little piles of junk. Before their unbelieving eyes, their villages, anchors of their very identity, were transformed into litter.

If they tried to flee as fish, Mac V of the Hosts turned the water into boiling oil. If they pretended to be trees, Mac V became a wind of fire. Confounded, they wept and died.

When it was done, Mac V put his ear to the forest. What he heard was not the sound of victory. He realized that most of the villages had been lost before the war began.

In Washington, they wanted only graphs. In Saigon, reporters joked that noodle restaurants were wrapping chicken in the Hamlet Evaluation Reports.

Binh Dinh Province, 1967. Vietnamese villagers, torn from their ancestral homelands by the war, become refugees in their own country.

Left. A sapper's-eye-view of a fortified village's outer defenses, south of Saigon, 1962. The fortified village was the South Vietnamese government's method of controlling the rural population, keeping the enemy out and rural civilians in.

Above. Montagnards of the central highlands examine their U.S.-supplied rifles, 1965. The montagnards, an ethnic minority in South Vietnam, were recruited by both U.S. Special Forces and the Communists.

Supporters of the Communist National Liberation Front (NLF) gather at the entrance to their village's tunnel network. The white headbands are symbols of mourning.

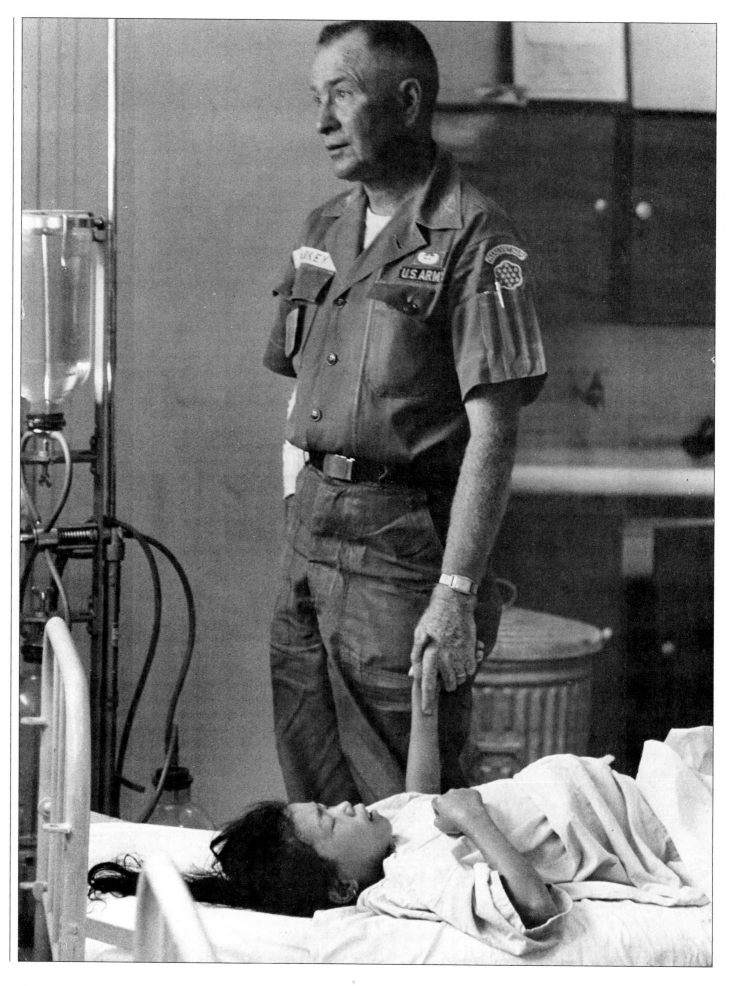

Left. In the My Tho village hospital south of Saigon, a U.S. Army doctor comforts a wounded child. The girl, Le Thi Lan (``Little Orchid''), struck by shrapnel from a hand grenade tossed into a busy market, died soon after surgery.

In a small Mekong Delta town, a little girl and a soldier of the U.S. 9th Division sit together.

Peasants in a Mekong Delta field continue their work as a bomb explodes nearby.

Above. U.S. Marines round up Vietcong suspects in Thanh Phong, a district of Kien Hoa Province, in January 1967.

Right, above and below. Clutching their children, two women escape their smoldering village on Cape Batangan in November 1965. The village was caught in a U.S. Marine attack, Operation Piranha. Before attacking, the Marines had issued warnings to evacuate but not all the villagers heard or heeded the Marines.

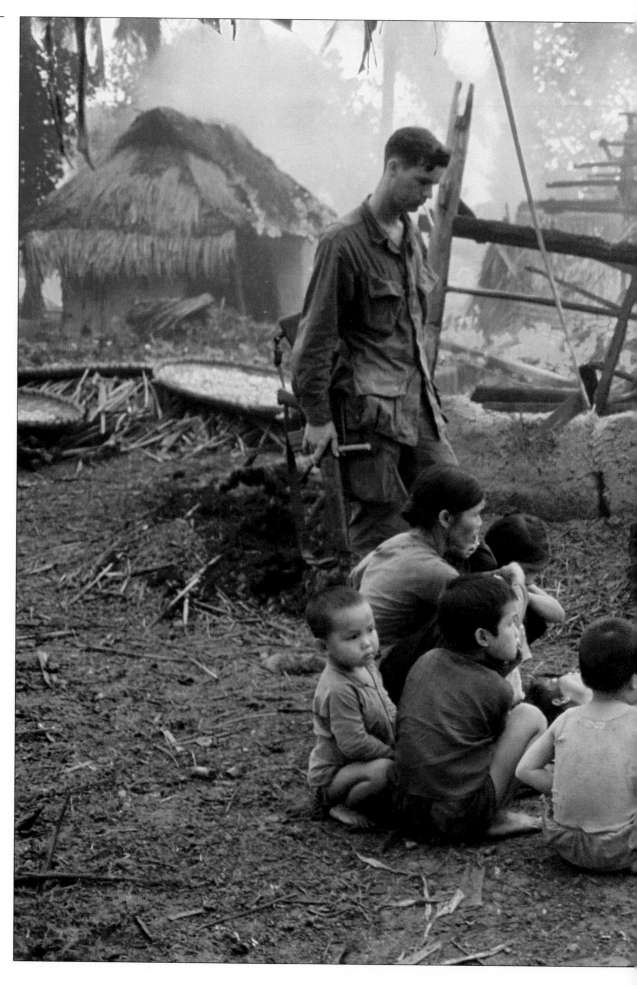

Children and other villagers sit in the ruins of their hamlet after a napalm attack, November 1967.

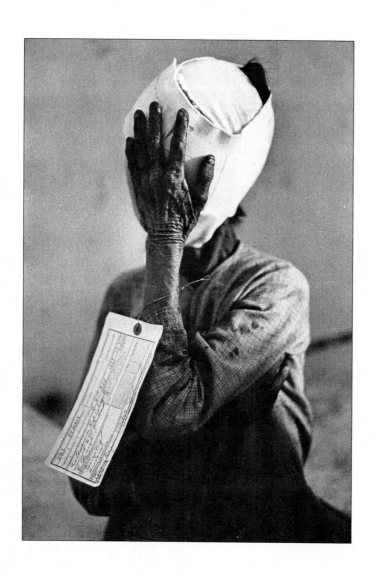

Above. A victim of war, Quang Ngai Province. The tag bears instructions that suggest how the person's wounds should be treated.

Right. Years after the war ended, the land remained scarred. This field, once a thick mangrove swamp, was decimated by the defoliant Agent Orange during an American sweep through the Ca Mau Peninsula.

Strategy of Attrition

The big battles before Tet may have been the last battles fought by American soldiers of the old style. The America they came from is not the same. Gone is the unambiguous, unembarrassed patriotism that sent so many of them to Vietnam. The senior officers and many of the senior noncoms had seen something of what the youngsters referred to as Double U Double U Deuce. More had been in Korea. The average infantryman in those days had gone in believing that you owed a service to your country, and, even though Double U Double U Deuce was an old black-and-white movie to him, he believed that being out there, fighting, surviving, and dying in those twenty-shades-of-nightmare-green places was the discharging of a natural debt.

They were the young men who had always turned out when assured the nation needed them, yet another generation of American fighting man, succeeding their fathers and older brothers as those in turn had succeeded theirs. They were the inheritors of a long tradition of righteousness and victory.

Their adolescent swagger concealed both conviction and self-doubt. Conviction was their birthright, after all. They were quite certain that they were in Vietnam to assist the common people in a struggle against hated foreign invaders from the North. They had been told this and they believed it. They had confidence in the men who led their country and its armed forces, but secretly their confidence in themselves was quite often a little shaky.

Their overall superior in Saigon was a Southerner, a former Eagle Scout from a family with a long military tradition. When asked if he could do a job, his in-stinct was to affirm vigorously that he could. That was the American way. Americans were winners.

General Westmoreland was not a sophisticated man, and he appears not to have realized how gravely the cards were stacked against him. His approach reflected a military philosophy, unique to the United States, which held that war was somehow a nonpolitical event. This philosophy had its roots in a salutary tradition excluding the armed forces from political involvement. The results of this tradition did not always serve the national interest. In World War II, to Churchill's consternation and Stalin's bemusement, American troops made no attempt to reach Berlin before the Russians, or to establish a Western military presence in central Europe. Eisenhower, acting on General Marshall's orders, declared that political considerations would not be allowed to influence military operations. Such a statement was utterly nonsensical to the war leaders of Europe, but most American soldiers accepted its soundness.

That the leading soldiers of a country born in insurrection should subscribe to such a doctrine is ironic, but Westmoreland, like his predecessors, did so. In the case of Vietnam, he could not have been more mistaken.

The enemy fought for precisely defined goals. Westmoreland served an administration whose war aims were so bound to political restrictions, foreign and domestic, that they could never be clarified beyond a generalized desire for good news. What state of affairs was he expected to bring about in Vietnam? Did he ever ask? The techno-maniacs and politicians to whom he reported never took the political risk of telling him. Sometimes they seemed to behave as though the Vietnam War was his idea and had nothing to do with them.

His declared tactics of search and destroy—finding and eliminating the enemy's main force—turned to rubble in his hands. He failed to gain the initiative at the outset and would never, in his years in Vietnam, succeed in attaining it. The strategy he employed would one day be described by some military historians as no strategy at all. Eventually, on the highest levels, everybody was faking it.

Out in the boondocks they were not faking it. At Dak To, and Bong Son, in the A Shau and Ia Drang valleys they were giving everything they had against a barely seen enemy deploying what may have been the best army of its time. They understood that they were not universally welcomed as liberators and that the enemy might be any Vietnamese, that the distinction between civilian and hostile combatant was obscure. They found themselves going short of food and water for fifty hours at a time because the choppers couldn't find a path through enemy fire, taking objectives at grave cost and abandoning them because there was no line of battle. They were ceasing to be what they had been, surprising themselves with their own endurance and sometimes with their own brutality. They were beginning to trust no one but each other.

Two soldiers of the 173d Airborne Brigade search for signs of the enemy during a sweep through the Iron Triangle, a Vietcong stronghold northwest of Saigon, 1965.

U.S.-trained soldiers of the Army of the Republic of Vietnam (ARVN) move past a hut they set afire after discovering Communist literature inside, 1963.

The bodies of NLF guerrillas lie next to an NLF flag in the Mekong Delta, 1962. At rear are American advisers and NLF prisoners. Even though its real value was uncertain, the "body count" became an important measure of U.S. progress in the war.

South Vietnamese
Marines, ferried in by
U.S.-supplied and
-piloted helicopters,
conduct a sweep for
the enemy in the rice
fields of the Mekong
Delta, early 1962.

American air power teamed with ground forces to seek out and destroy the enemy and his support system. *Above.* An F-4C Phantom jet fires its rockets at a Vietcong-controlled village.

Opposite above. Napalm inflames a village after a strike by an A-1 Skyraider.

Opposite below. Smoke enshrouds huts in an enemy village after an airstrike.

Left. His eyes and mouth taped shut, a Vietcong guerrilla captured during Operation Piranha awaits his fate. The operation was carried out to destroy elements of the Vietcong on Cape Batangan, east of Chu Lai, in November 1965.

Above. A weary American soldier, a member of a "Zippo" squad (so called by the soldiers because of the squad's assignment), breaks for a cigarette after evacuating and burning a village in Quang Ngai Province, 1967. The village was completely destroyed to deny its use by the enemy.

Male villagers are led off to imprisonment and interrogation in Binh Dinh Province, 1966. They are suspected of being members of the Vietcong.

Left. A wounded Marine of the 3d Battalion, 4th Marines, is carried to an air evacuation point by two comrades during the battle for Hill 484, an insignificant peak just below the demilitarized zone. The battle was one of the fiercest of Operation Prairie, in which Marines pushed an invading NVA division out of South Vietnam's northern provinces in late 1966.

Above. An officer (left) shouts orders to the men of Company B, 4th Battalion, 503d Infantry, during the battle for Hill 875. The unit was deployed during search and destroy operations around Dak To in late 1967 to relieve the badly mauled 2d Battalion.

Nineteen-year-old Vernon Wike, a navy corpsman, tries vainly to save the life of an injured Marine during the battle of Hill 881 North. After applying a compress to a chest wound (opposite above), Wike realizes that the soldier is dead (opposite below). The corpsman then searches the area for other wounded under fire (above). The twelve-day battle to clear the Khe Sanh Valley of NVA regulars took place in the spring of 1967.

Taps. Ninety-eight pairs of empty combat boots bear silent witness to the 173d Air-borne's casualties from the battle for Hill 875. Survivors stand at attention as the names of the dead are read aloud.

The Other Side

In Vietnam, one's choice of words when referring to the enemy defined one's attitude toward the war. This was true of the servicemen and also of the civilians there, the press corps, the AID people, the contractors, social workers, and spooks.

The lowest term for the NLF, so low that it indicated a baseness of character on the user's part, was, "The Cong." This was the term favored by the *New York Daily News*. It was employed by right-wing American civil servants and by certain visiting politicians who came over to be photographed in the act of "fact-finding." They would use the degrading term in conversation with the troops they wanted to be photographed among, imagining that it made them one of the guys. A politician who referred to "The Cong" was sure to find facts supportive of a continuing effort. The term "The Cong" was also used archly by those well out of the line.

"Vietcong," originally a derogatory reference in Vietnamese, was more or less neutral; its users often incorrectly applied it to include NVA regulars. "Charlie" was in general use, but it presumed an actual acquaintance with the enemy and sounded fatuous from anyone who had never heard an AK47. "Victor Charlie" was straight phonetic alphabet, less familiar and preferred. Civilians and others who wanted to sound serious referred to "Victor Charles." Black soldiers, to whom "Charlie" was somebody else back home, often spoke of plain "Charles."

In the line, where the general feeling held that a gook was a gook, the term "gook" was applied to all Vietnamese, hostile, friendly, or stoically indifferent. Superstitious short-timers and admiring soldiers spoke of "Sir Charles" or even "Charles, sir" and applied it to all enemy combatants. Quakers, Third Country nationals, and left-wing journalists referred to "The Front," meaning the Communist-led National Liberation Front.

It was declared a great mystery that Vietnamese in the VC and NVA fought so furiously and well while our ARVN allies so often performed poorly. The answer, as everyone well knew, was motivation and leadership.

The sacrifices expected of a VC or NVA soldier were awe-inspiring. That they were, in general, performed was more so. Their leadership was not conservative of their lives; the acceptable casualty rate in the NVA was higher than that in the Japanese army during World War II. General Giap's statement has often been quoted: "Every minute hundreds of thousands of people die on this earth. The life and death of a hundred, a thousand, tens of thousands of human beings, even our compatriots, means little."

Over here we try not to think like that. The general sounds to our ears like a wartime movie villain, confirming the old saw about Asians and the value of life. Yet his troops behaved as though they agreed with him. Living in unlivable jungle, often without medicine or hope of rescue if injured, without fires to cook or warm themselves from the night's chill, without word of their families, they went out to scatter their lives like pebbles.

"Can it be just *dulce et decorum est?*" someone once asked during a bull session in some safe place.

"What else can it be?" someone else answered by asking.

Dulce et decorum est pro patria mori. Sweet and righteous it is to die for the fatherland.

A modern poet has called that motto an "old lie." Many Americans once believed it, or at least it did not seem to them altogether impossible.

Some of the unsophisticated among the first troops we sent to Vietnam believed it. It quickly became a sick joke, or would have if anyone had had the nerve to recite it on the line.

But to the other side it was a religion. Their soldiers didn't die for the dialectic or for the thesis on State and Revolution. They lived in an ordered world long lost to us for good or ill. They believed what they were told, and they believed their lives belonged to the land and to the people. Their naive faith made them the hardest and most determined enemy America ever faced.

Vietcong guerrillas cross a clearing while on patrol in a South Vietnamese jungle, May 1965. They carry French submachine guns and rice packed in sacks made of U.S. parachute silk.

The Vietcong used an elaborate system of tunnels and underground bunkers for protection and resupply, including this one, located near Saigon, 1967. In the foreground is a Russian-made rocket propelled grenade launcher.

Left. North Vietnamese President Ho Chi
Minh (left) and Prime Minister Pham Van
Dong confer in the garden of the former
palace of the French governor-general in
Hanoi, November 1968. Ho, president of
North Vietnam for twenty-four years, died
the following September.

Above. North Vietnamese soldiers work on
a Soviet-supplied surface-to-air missile
(SAM). The advanced antiaircraft system
around Hanoi and Haiphong, which employed SAMs and a variety of antiaircraft
artillery, was the most effective Americans
had ever faced.

Trucks filled with supplies for the fighting in the South cross a stream along the Ho Chi Minh Trail, the complex of paths and roads extending throughout the border regions of Laos and Cambodia. Bridges were sometimes constructed inches beneath water level to conceal them from American reconnaissance aircraft.

During the 1968 Tet offensive, the Vietcong joined North Vietnamese regulars in attacks on South Vietnam's major population centers. Left. A female VC guerrilla carrying a load of ammunition dives for cover when the area is shelled.

Above. An NVA soldier aims his Soviet-made light machine gun over a pile of rubble during the assault on Hue during the Tet offensive. The Communists captured and held the former imperial capital for several weeks.

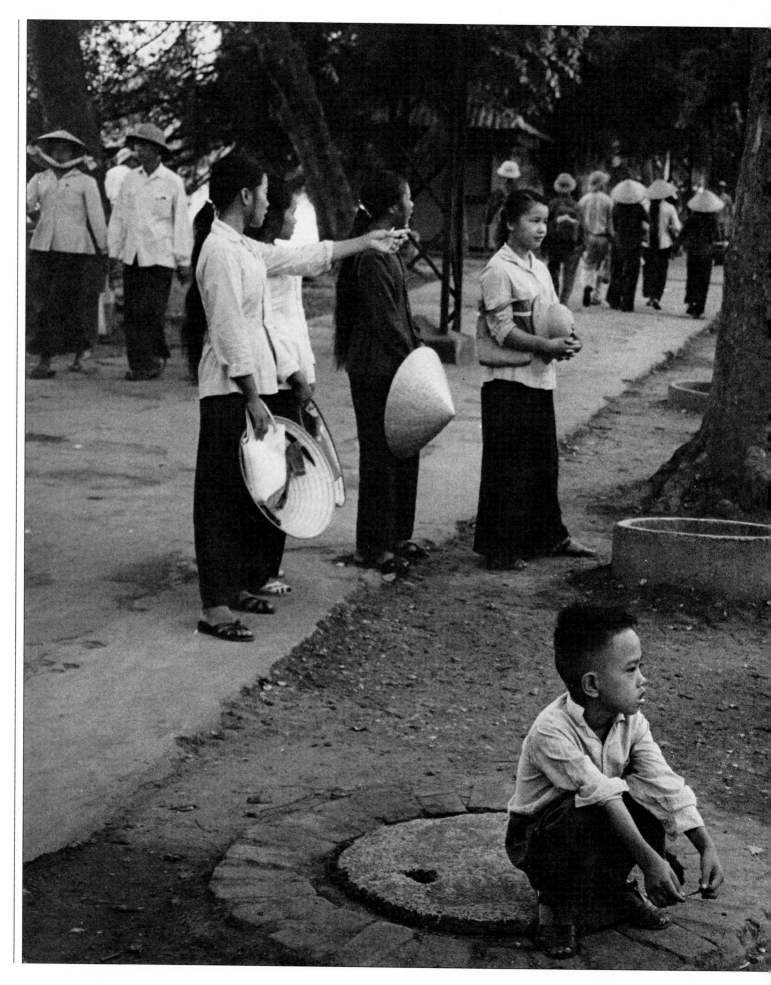

After President Johnson halted the bombing of the North in 1968, Hanoi's streets filled with people, including a young boy perched on the cover of a manhole bomb shelter. Because of the American bombings, one-third to one-half of the city's population had been evacuated to rural areas starting in June 1965.

Above left. Madame Nguyen Thi Binh, PRG foreign minister and the official PRG representative to the Paris peace talks. The daughter of a Vietnamese nationalist, Binh started her career in 1950 by resisting French rule.

Above right. General Vo Nguyen Giap, North Vietnam's minister of defense, planned both the victory against the French at Dien Bien Phu in 1954 and the Tet offensive of 1968.

Left. U.S. Air Force Major Dewey Waddell is led to prison after being shot down and captured by North Vietnamese civilian militia, April 1968.

Cho Sat market in the port city of Haiphong lies in ruins after a bombing raid by U.S. aircraft on April 16, 1972. The bombing was part of Operation Linebacker I, a series of raids carried out in retaliation for the North's Easter offensive of 1972.

Khe Sanh

Who won what at Khe Sanh remains obscure. Both sides claim it as a victory. It was a remote battlefield, either strategically vital or nowhere at all. Its value depended on the strategic perspective, the personal interest, or the public relations position of the evaluator.

Were the Marines sent there to hold the "western anchor" of South Vietnam's defenses and close the Ho Chi Minh Trail? Or were they there as bait to draw the Communists into a conventional battle in which their army might be destroyed by superior fire and air power? Or were the NVA divisions themselves the bait, there to lure American forces into an unoccupied corner of the country while the Tet offensive struck at the centers of population? Were the NVA forces repulsed in their determined attempt to inflict a major defeat on the United States? Or was their effort a feint to distract MACV's attention from plans for the more strategically important assaults?

For the strategists in Saigon, Honolulu, and Washington, Khe Sanh became a state of mind. Lyndon Johnson, master of persuasion and hyperbole, dreaded the reaction of the press and the Congress to a setback there. Above all he dreaded the reaction of the public whose love and admiration he required.

Dreadful analogies suggested themselves. The words *Dien Bien Phu* were uttered. The public read those words and heard them on television. *Dien Bien Phu*, horrible words, dust on the tongue, mud, defeat, capitulation. Incomprehensible words, the name of a place to buy opium and of a foreign army's destruction, became a symbol of that land war in Asia America had been cautioned against since MacArthur's day. Its shadow fell across time and distance to dishearten the country's war leaders.

Sleepless and haggard, Johnson paced the White House situation room. A sand reproduction of Khe Sanh had been built for his benefit. He read and tried to interpret every incoming dispatch. He was squandering the last of his optimism, energy, and determination. As the siege wore on and the reports of the Tet offensive kept coming, Johnson's writers struggled for the right words of explanation. Seen from Washington or even Saigon, the situation was complex.

For the 6,000 Marines and 300 ARVN Rangers inside the Khe Sanh perimeter the situation was elemental. Ranged against them were up to four divisions of North Vietnam's regular army equipped with heavy guns and even tanks. For seventy-seven days, between the end of January and early April 1968, the men at Khe Sanh endured a sustained attack that ceased to be an event with cause, beginning, and foreseeable end but became a condition of life to which the only alternative was death.

They never got a glimpse of the Big Picture. There were only small pictures, moments of fire, pain, and sudden death. Only those who were there can really know what it was like.

One who was there was the great war photographer David Duncan, who shared the Marines' ordeal and who took the pictures that follow. Combat troops often asked journalists why the writers were in the line. Duncan has answered most eloquently in words he wrote after covering the war in Korea and used again at Khe Sanh to explain his business.

"I wanted to show what war does to a man," Duncan wrote. "I wanted to show the comradeship that binds men together when they are fighting a common peril. I wanted to show the way men live, and die, when they know death is among them, and yet they still find the strength to crawl forward armed only with bayonets to stop the advance of men they have never seen, with whom they have no immediate quarrel, men who will kill them on sight if given first chance. I wanted to show the agony, the suffering, the terrible confusion, the heroism which is everyday currency among those men who actually pull the triggers of rifles aimed at other men known as 'the enemy.' I wanted to tell a story of war, as war has always been for men. Only their weapons, the terrain, the causes have changed."

Nearly 500 Marines died defending Khe Sanh and perhaps 10,000 North Vietnamese soldiers assaulting the place were killed or wounded. But the war, in its perversity, had a way of denying the most valiant the fruits of their valor. Once the fighting was over, the dead of both sides buried, and the wounded removed to where they might be healed, Khe Sanh had no attraction for either side. General Westmoreland ordered the base dismantled.

A soldier of Echo Company, 26th Marines, buries his face in a Bible after surviving the battle for Hill 861 Alpha. The hilltop outpost near Khe Sanh was attacked by NVA soldiers on January 21, 1968.

Two Marines at Khe Sanh mark time in a fog-enshrouded bunker. Bad weather hampered resupply efforts throughout the seventy-seven-day siege of Khe Sanh.

Above. Only one C-130 transport plane was lost to enemy fire during the siege of Khe Sanh. The plane, piloted by Chief Warrant Officer Harry Wildfang, a veteran of both World War II and Korea, was struck by machine-gun fire that ignited its cargo of aviation fuel as it touched down on the metal runway. Opposite above. Fire-fighters attempted to control the flames from the C-130 with foam, to no avail, leaving them with the grim task of sifting through the wreckage for bodies. Opposite below. As the burning hulk of the plane cools, the fire crew chief stands amid the rubble. Wildfang and his copilot survived, but six others aboard the plane were killed.

A sniper team of Company E, 2d Battalion, 26th Marines, picks out enemy targets on Hill 861 Alpha, an outpost on the perimeter of Khe Sanh. As Lance Corporal Albert Miranda draws a bead, Lance Corporal David Burdwell points out an enemy soldier to Lieutenant Alec Bodenwiser.

A soldier of the 26th Marines picks his way through enemy bodies on Hill 861 Alpha, the scene of bloody hand-to-hand clashes in the early days of the siege.

As clouds and fog close in on the mountains surrounding Khe Sanh, a squad of Marines lifts the bodies of American casualties into a CH–47 Chinook helicopter.

Tet!

Vietnamese tradition held that the turning of the lunar year should bring auspicious signs and gladness of heart; thus it had become customary for both sides to observe a truce during the holiday celebrations. In 1968, a thirty-six-hour cease-fire had been agreed upon, to commence at midnight on January 30.

Centuries before, Vietnam had won a great victory in her running war with the Chinese by attacking their Hanoi garrison at the height of the Tet observances. In 1968, the Communist-led forces in Vietnam chose to create their own auspicious signs by repeating history.

A little after midnight on January 30, they assaulted the Nha Trang perimeter. All day long, from Quang Tri to Ca Mau, in a barrage of rockets and mortars, they attacked provincial capitals and divisional headquarters. No target was too formidable. They attacked Bien Hoa, Cam Ranh Bay, and even Tan Son Nhut. Vietcong and NVA soldiers were fighting in the streets of Hue, Da Nang, and Saigon itself.

In a sense, the Tet battles of 1968 saw both sides fall victim to their own propaganda. When NVA divisions began converging around the combat base at Khe Sanh in early January, President Johnson worried about a "second Dien Bien Phu." MACV welcomed the prospect. According to his body-count scorekeeping, the enemy was on the ropes. Dien Bien Phu would be refought and he would win it. He threw the bulk of his combat maneu-

verables into I Corps to engage NVA regulars. By the morning of January 31 "The Front" was outside his back window, F-100s were flying tactical air support over the streets of Saigon, and there were firefights in progress on the U.S. Embassy lawn. The ARVN had gone on holiday routine.

But all was not going according to plan for the attackers. They found no "general uprising" to welcome their "general offensive." Confident of victory and conscious of history, Communist guerrillas fought their way into every city in the country and foundered there, fish out of water. Whether they acted as a matter of policy or out of frustration at their compatriots' lack of ardor, some of the worst atrocities charged to their account occurred during the twenty-six days they held power in sections of Hue. Afterward, more than 3,000 bodies were found in mass graves around the city. Some had been buried alive.

After the fact, MACV would take comfort from the enormous numbers of enemy dead. His spokesmen would call the Tet offensive a "last ditch struggle" and compare it to the German winter offensive of 1944. But something was wrong. It became apparent that the enemy had taken MACV by surprise. His spokesmen said contradictory things about the enemy's intentions. His own intentions were unclear. He seemed not to be in control. He was fighting the enemy's war in the enemy's good time. If the enemy chose to fight on

MACV's front porch, the enemy had the capability. If the enemy chose western Quang Tri Province MACV would hasten to meet him there.

With Tet, Vietnam finally got America's attention. Millions of Americans watched the battle for Saigon on the evening news, and many who were not personally involved took notice for the first time. In the winter dusk of America as 1968 proceeded, dreadful sights were broadcast. The cameras recorded burnings, executions, even the sight of American soldiers falling in battle. MACV was powerless to control news media that no longer trusted him. He had sincerely believed there would be nothing to hide.

Lyndon Johnson tried to explain it away and his own credibility suffered. On February 27, the avuncular Walter Cronkite, a public surrogate, pondered the question of whether "the bloody experience of Vietnam is to end in stalemate." The decade that had opened in the winter sunshine of Kennedy's inaugural was flickering out in a confusion of shadows and unwholesome light.

Two American Marines battle Communist troops inside the walls of the Citadel at Hue. The former imperial capital was overrun by the enemy, then retaken by Marines during the Tet offensive of 1968.

South Vietnamese soldiers hunker down as a street on the outskirts of Saigon becomes an inferno, February 8, 1968. The fighting in Saigon began with attacks on January 31, 1968, and lasted into the second week of February.

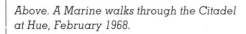

Above. A Marine walks through the Citadel at Hue, February 1968.

Right. Under fire from a Vietcong machine gun, American Marines run for cover south of the Perfume River near Hue.

Left. Americans hastily drag away the body of a comrade killed during a VC attack near Tan Son Nhut Airport on January 31, 1968. The VC made a direct hit on a truckload of MPs, then raked the area with automatic fire as survivors dived for cover.

Above. A young boy grieves over the body of his sister, killed by U.S. helicopter gunfire near the Y Bridge when fighting again terrorized Saigon during "mini-Tet," May 1968.

Left. Two Marines take shelter against incoming shells in Hue during the Tet offensive.

Above. Wounded in crossfire during the
battle for Hue, a child is carried from the
front by an American medic.

Above. North Vietnamese soldiers in Hue guard a position with Chinese-made AK47 rifles. To photograph NVA units, French photographer Catherine Leroy worked her way behind Communist lines during the battle.

Right. Marines interrogate a Vietnamese civilian captured in Hue during Tet 1968. Many civilians were suspected of having collaborated with the NVA to pave the way for the offensive.

Above. Hue aftermath. In downtown Hue, survivors watch a victim of the fighting float down a canal.

Right. The imperial palace at Hue lies ravaged after the fierce fighting to recapture the city.

Above. A woman weeps over the remains of her husband, killed at Hue in the Tet offensive. The body, along with hundreds of others apparently slain by the Communists, was discovered in a shallow mass grave outside the city more than a year after the Tet battle.

Right. A North Vietnamese soldier slain in the battle for Hue lies surrounded by personal effects scattered by plundering soldiers.

War at Home

In the autumn of 1961, I was working as a house painter in a cavernous apartment on Central Park West. Over some hipster station on my radio, a man with an impenetrable foreign accent was engaged in a diatribe against American policy in Southeast Asia. I let him ramble on until I had second-coated a corner lintel, then I climbed down my ladder and turned the dial in search of something with a better beat. I didn't want to hear it.

Not many years later, at the street separating Oakland, California, from Berkeley, I saw the Oakland cops open their ranks to let some Hell's Angels get at the marchers in a demonstration against the Vietnam War, while the Berkeley Police—responsible public servants with degrees in law enforcement—tried to fight off the bikers. A couple of years after that, the conflict between authority and protest had grown so intense that the Berkeley Police were discharging bird shot into demonstrators' faces, friends of mine were in jail or being chased by the FBI, and I got beaten up in High Spire, Pennsylvania, for having a beard.

And finally I was there, hiding at midday among the rubber trees and sliding dipthongs, trying to read myself into a paperback copy of *Nicholas and Alexandra* and out of Binh Duong Province and the Republic of Vietnam.

It seemed as though it would never go away. Now there are college students who don't know the first thing about it and a lot of people who wish they didn't either.

During the same years that President Kennedy was trying to find his way through the rococo politics of Vietnam, a new generation of the expanded American middle class was coming of age. There may be some principle by which powerful industrialized systems generate romantic revivals; in any case America had something very like one during the late fifties and early sixties. The generation coming up seemed to have no tolerance for the long-accepted scandals and the dirty secrets America had always lived with. Reinhold Niebuhr, a cold war theologian and a pessimist, had preached an imperfect world in which one measure of a nation's strength was its ability to reconcile itself to inevitable injustices. The middle-class young of the sixties felt it was their responsibility to change the world and to reconcile American rhetoric with American reality. Born to relative security in a powerful country, they felt firm ground beneath their feet, and they thought they saw very clearly what should be changed. They were witnessing the dismantling of institutionalized racism; some of them had taken part in that process.

John Kennedy was shot down before their eyes. When Lyndon Johnson mistook his election for more than a mandate and began leading the country into a foreign war, they would not follow him. When he lied, a new generation of journalists and teachers was ready to expose his stratagems. Their opposition became more obstreperous and more offensive. They were ready to listen to radical counsels that had been suppressed in the fifties. They

were ready to develop a radicalism of their own. A mass bohemia came into being, despising those outside it and becoming despised in turn.

If the administration was going to win its war in Vietnam, it needed to do so quickly and unambiguously. Lacking clear objectives, it was bound to fail. Johnson's good intentions and social idealism disappeared in a chorus of shouted obscenities. Because of the war, America would never love or honor him in the way that he required. The road to hell is paved with good intentions.

The part of America that was not young or middle class—those who had always known you got nothing for nothing, you got what you could, you were lucky to get what you worked for—turned coldly nihilistic. It was hard to tell which they hated more—the war or its opponents. Selective service was in effect raiding the towns and the ghettos. Little flags were whipping on the wind in mean cemeteries from the New England mill towns to the Southern Pacific tracks.

Where love and peace failed, grief, bitterness, and disillusionment prevailed. The youthful rapture ended and Nixon seemed to be president after all. Nixon, who did not care much for causes, eventually brought the boys home.

President John F. Kennedy at his inauguration on January 20, 1961. In his address, the young president summoned the nation to "pay any price, bear any burden . . . to assure the survival and the success of liberty" throughout the world.

On April 17, 1965, thousands of students from around the country gathered on the Mall in Washington, D.C., to protest the growing U.S. involvement in Vietnam. The demonstration, organized by the Students for a Democratic Society (SDS), was the largest held in Washington up to that time.

Above. A demonstrator places pink carnations in MP's rifle barrels during the antiwar March on the Pentagon, October 1967. Violence erupted soon afterward; scores of demonstrators were injured and hundreds arrested during a weekend of protest.

Right. Supporters of the war in Vietnam stage a demonstration in New York City in response to an antiwar march up Fifth Avenue to Central Park in September 1968. Until 1968, more Americans favored the war than opposed it.

Above. The shock of assassination added fuel to the growing fires of national unrest. Four days after Martin Luther King, Jr., was shot to death in Memphis, his widow, Coretta Scott King, embraces their daughter during funeral services for the civil rights leader in Atlanta on April 9, 1968.

Right. Two months after King's death, on June 5, 1968, Senator Robert Kennedy lies dying in the dim light of a Los Angeles hotel kitchen as a busboy, Juan Romero, kneels beside him. Kennedy had been a vocal critic of President Lyndon Johnson's Vietnam policy.

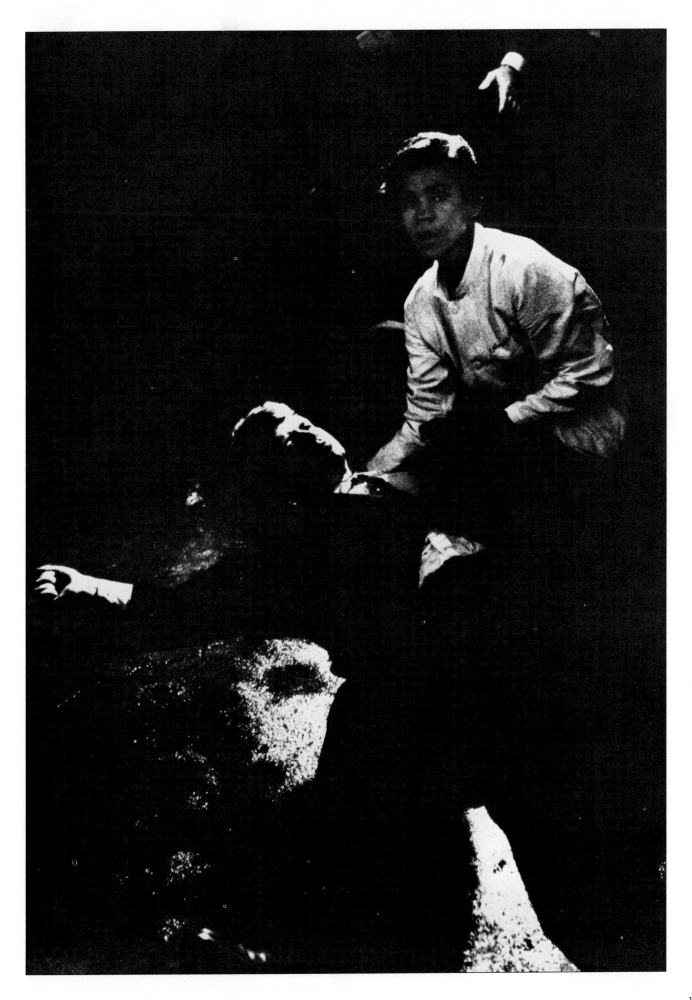

Above. Corporal Perron Shinneman, who lost a leg in Vietnam, is welcomed home by his wife Shirley in Sioux Falls, South Dakota, on August 13, 1966.

Right. President Lyndon B. Johnson is overcome with emotion as he listens to a tape recording of his son-in-law describing the hardship of war while on duty in Vietnam. Johnson decided not to seek reelection in 1968 primarily because of the Vietnam quagmire.

Left. At the 1968 Democratic National Convention in Chicago, Mayor Richard Daley unleashed the city's police against antiwar demonstrators. Here he leads supporters in a cheer for his hard-line stance.

Above. Enraged at police who have already beaten and arrested other antiwar demonstrators, a crowd taunts a line of officers on Michigan Avenue, outside the Democratic Convention.

Swinging billy clubs, Chicago police wade into a crowd of anti-war demonstrators in Grant Park on August 28, 1968. The actions of law enforcement officials during the Democratic National Convention were later characterized as a "police riot."

Left. In May 1970, construction workers in New York City march in support of President Richard Nixon's Vietnam policy. "Hard hats," who mounted demonstrations throughout the war, were the most visible representatives of prowar sentiment.

Above. In Berkeley, an antiwar demonstrator throws a tear gas canister back at police during a protest against the 1970 U.S. incursion into Cambodia. Nixon's move into Cambodia was greeted by protests around the nation.

Vietnam veterans opposed to the war demonstrate in Washington, D.C., during "Operation Dewey Canyon III" in April 1971. The demonstration, named after Marine operations in Laos, was called "a limited incursion into the country of Congress."

Left. Antiwar demonstrators hold a candle-light vigil in New York City's Washington Square Park, December 1969.

Above. President Nixon and National Security Adviser Henry Kissinger confer in the White House garden on September 16, 1972. Both men scorned the antiwar protests, yet moved to end the war.

144

Left. War touches Massilon, Ohio. On June 25, 1966, a boy pauses to watch the funeral of Private First Class Robert Damian Wuertz, Jr., the first man from Massilon killed in the war.

Above. Two Vietnam veterans console each other during antiwar protests in Harrisburg, Pennsylvania in September 1971.

Withdrawal

At the Five O'clock Follies, as the press called the daily MACV briefing, officers continued to refer to American and ARVN troops as the *Allies:* The term made reporters wince because it seemed so transparently a forlorn attempt to invoke the sense of relentless moral and military victory that accompanied World War II's closing days. Beyond their attempts at homespun agitprop, MACV's spokesmen had little to report by May 1971. Like tragedians in a bad melodrama, they tried hard not to be laughed at; they had learned what the laugh lines were and avoided them.

The Big Story was Vietnamization, which was to enter its second phase during the coming summer. Lam Son 719, ARVN's solo incursion into Laos earlier that spring, had been a substantial test of Vietnamization, America's plans to turn the fighting over to the South Vietnamese.

When that operation was over, President Nixon addressed America in a televised speech in which he declared: "Tonight I can report that Vietnamization has succeeded." His words reflected MACV's official judgment, but the enduring image of Lam Son 719 was a photograph of a South Vietnamese soldier clinging to the skid of a medevac chopper during ARVN's frantic withdrawal. Everything had gone wrong. Bad weather had grounded air support and prevented preparatory attacks. Bad intelligence had resulted in the ARVN raiders facing superior numbers, superior artillery, and a large, well-coordinated tank force. ARVNs had even been bombed mistakenly by the United States Navy while forming up.

In Saigon, MACV took the long view. His statistics led him to conclude that "the NVA had taken another beating." Issues of *Time, Newsweek,* and other publications reporting the extent of the debacle were banned by Thieu's government.

The Corsican proprietor of my hotel professed to believe that America would change sides to win. The U.S. was in the war for oil, he believed. It would abandon Thieu and cut a deal with Hanoi—that, he insisted, was what the Paris peace talks were about.

Rumors of American accommodation with the enemy spread, and some Vietnamese hastened to make accommodations of their own. We heard that one of the Vietcong cadres in Saigon had absconded with a fortune in "tax" money. All over the country government authorities approached their Communist opposite numbers, and arrangements for peaceful coexistence were worked out.

Meanwhile, the U.S. military was going through a crisis. Fraggings of officers and noncoms by their troops and refusals of combat seemed to be increasing, but it was hard to tell how frequently they occurred. If the Public Affairs people knew, they weren't letting on. A group of young lawyers was dispatched from Harvard Law School to defend court-martial defendants—the antiwar movement was showing its colors in Saigon.

According to some, the seeds of a large-scale mutiny were sprouting in line units. Others claimed this was gross ex- aggeration. But it was plain that soldiers called upon to risk their lives in a war they knew held no prospect of victory were angry and frustrated, reflecting attitudes at home. The doctrine of Black Power had arrived in Vietnam, and race relations in the rear echelons ranged from tense to deadly. MACV got his soldiers back to The World as fast as he dared.

The spring of 1971 seemed the beginning of the end and so—as things turned out—it was. Reporters began to speculate, privately, on what the inevitable Communist victory would mean for South Vietnam. There was a story in neighboring Cambodia; few knew much about what was happening there. Those who had known were dead.

Demoralization in Saigon was visible; the city was febrile with early symptoms of terminal defeat. Many thousands of poor refugees from American bombs and NVA mortars had jammed into the capital, hopelessly overstraining its capacity to house or employ them. As Vietnamization proceeded, individual Americans began to ponder the circumstances of their own private withdrawal.

The base camp of the U.S. 11th Armored Cavalry near Snuol, Cambodia, May 1970. The invasion of NVA sanctuaries in Cambodia provoked public outcry in the U.S. and raised doubts about Nixon's program to end the war. The U.S.–South Vietnamese invaders captured or destroyed large amounts of enemy supplies.

Left. Surrounded by the American troops he has promised to bring home as part of his plan to turn the war over to the South Vietnamese, President Richard M. Nixon tours the 1st Division's base camp at Di An, near Saigon, July 30, 1969.

Above. American GIs interrogate a Vietcong prisoner, 1969.

An American soldier turns a firebase heli-pad into a giant slate for antiwar graffiti near Qui Nhon, April 1972.

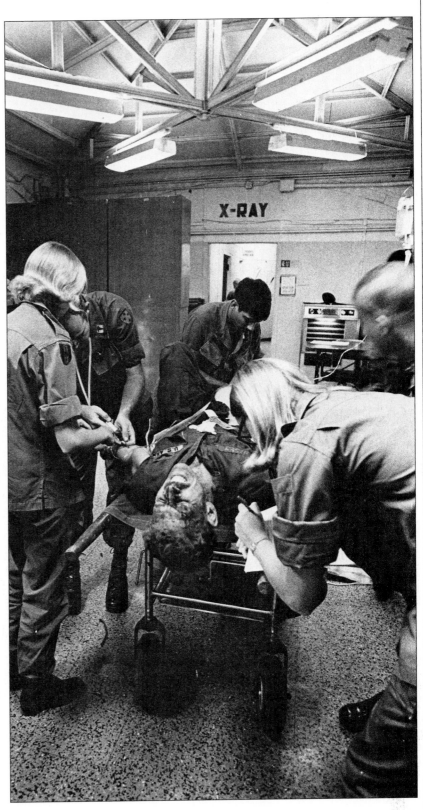

A medevac pilot whose helicopter crashed
in the Bien Hoa River receives emergency
medical attention at the 93d Evacuation
Hospital, Long Binh, on April 14, 1970.

Crewmen take a breather aboard the aircraft carrier U.S.S. Hancock. American airpower played a vital role in the Vietnamization process as navy, Marine, and air force pilots flew in support of South Vietnamese ground operations. More than once, and especially during the 1972 NVA Easter offensive, the American pilots saved the day for the ARVN.

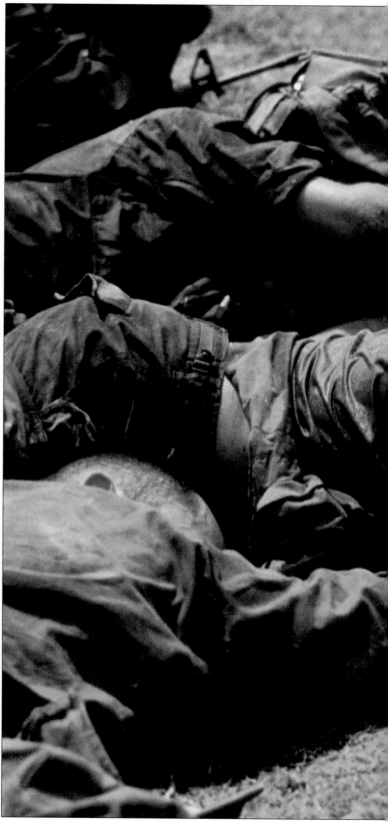

Above. Racial violence was sparked by the American and South Vietnamese invasion of Cambodia. Cambodian mobs attacked ethnic Vietnamese and their businesses, and Khmer troops massacred hundreds of Vietnamese. The U.S. and South Vietnamese eventually organized a flotilla that ferried Vietnamese civilians like this mother and child down the Mekong River into South Vietnam.

Right. An exhausted GI drinks from his canteen after collapsing in the searing heat of the Fishhook region on the Cambodia–South Vietnam border, May 1970.

Black soldiers in Vietnam, 1970. The emerging black consciousness movement in the U.S. Army reflected, in part, a sentiment against fighting a ``white man's war'' in Southeast Asia.

Faces of the disengagement army: GIs of the 1st Air Cavalry Division after a night-time firefight with enemy troops at Fire Support Base Wood, April 1970. The Americans fought Communist troops hand-to-hand but in the darkness and confusion also fired at each other.

A medevac helicopter arrives at Khe Sanh loaded with South Vietnamese wounded during Operation Lam Son 719, the South Vietnamese invasion of southern Laos, early 1971. The invasion, which had been advertised as a showcase of Vietnamization, turned into a rout of the ARVN after poor planning and ineffective leadership doomed the effort.

Above. A soldier makes a friend in Cholon, the Chinese district of Saigon.

Right. Part of the legacy of the American occupation of South Vietnam was children fathered by servicemen. An Amerasian child at a Saigon-area refugee center stands next to a school bell made from an old shell case, January 1973.

At the Paris peace talks, U.S. National Security Adviser Henry Kissinger shares a
joke with North Vietnamese negotiator Le
Duc Tho (right) and his deputy, Xuan Thuy,
(middle) in November 1972. In October,
Kissinger had prematurely announced
"peace is at hand." The talks deadlocked
in December, and Nixon ordered a mas-
sive air offensive against North Vietnam in
December 1972.

In January 1973, North Vietnamese civilians stand near the wreckage of an American B–52 bomber that was shot down during the "Christmas bombings" of the North. Thousands of North Vietnamese civilians were killed during the bombings, which caused international outrage at Nixon's tactics. The administration, however, credited the bombings with bringing the peace talks to a successful conclusion.

The Easter Offensive

When South Vietnamese elections came due in the autumn of 1971, the American Presence in Saigon rounded up the usual suspects and decided to stay with Nguyen Van Thieu. The customary CIA funds were disbursed to Thieu's faction. The customary victory of democracy was proclaimed.

It was entirely a matter of the lesser evil. Thieu was unsatisfactory in so many ways that the advantages of his continuance in office were largely negative. Under his leadership, the ARVN remained an instrument of patronage in which only political reliability was rewarded. It was highly unlikely, allowing for the luxuries of hindsight, that such a man leading such a government and army could succeed against a highly motivated force of practical fanatics. Vietnamization had been nearly discredited during Lam Son 719, but it was the only formula available. American officials and advisers, who on one level knew the state of things perfectly well, spoke optimistically as from a schizoid trance. Hanoi, having rebuilt its plants, its army, and defenses, and equipped by Communist superpowers competing for its allegiance, set out to show what it could do.

On March 30, 1972, the NVA struck on three fronts. One force came over the DMZ, a second into the central highlands, and a third into the Iron Triangle above Saigon. The suffering and devastation this "Easter offensive" inflicted on the South Vietnamese people may have been the most ghastly of the entire war. With siz-able cities under siege, the roads were clogged with refugees whose fear of living in the line of fire or under the Communists emboldened them to flee across an inferno. The very air was deadly. Families, carrying their possessions, made their way through massed NVA artillery which was firing up to 7,000 shells a day into the heavily populated city of An Loc. Exploding American bombs and naval gunfire from ships in the Tonkin Gulf added to the casualties along the road from Quang Tri. Route 1, between Quang Tri and Hue, came to be called the Highway of Terror, as it had long before been called the Street Without Joy.

The ARVN was leaderless. When facing insurgents in earlier times, it had been trained in conventional warfare. Then under General Creighton Abrams the American advisers had shifted emphasis to counterinsurgency, but by 1971 the enemy was employing tank units and heavy guns.

In the end, American advisers made the difference on the three fronts. Supported in large measure by American air power, the ARVN regained the shapeless, bloodstained wreckage that had been An Loc and Quang Tri. As in the past, Hanoi's offensive faded away, leaving "victors" who were decimated by casualties, exhausted, and more demoralized than ever.

President Nixon, facing protests in the U.S. and risking a diplomatic strategy that had invested his personal prestige in "détente" with the Communist super-powers, ordered North Vietnam bombed "as it had never been bombed before."

But Hanoi had made its point. The day was coming when Nguyen Van Thieu's Vietnam would be virtually on its own. Only U.S. air power stood between the regime and its mortal enemies. Vietnamization, essentially, had failed.

Rumors—and that is all they were—of secret accommodation between North Vietnam and America had first circulated after Tet, 1968. With every crisis they surfaced again, and after the Easter offensive they were heard everywhere and almost everywhere believed: Americans had allowed North Vietnamese troops into the cities; the Vietnamese had avoided killing Americans and killed ARVNs instead. The talk was always of what the Communists would do and above all of what the Americans would do.

Mac V, in his windowless office piled high with surveys, evaluations, and reports went out and saw that the war was lost. Saigon, a city now more dense with refugees than ever, turned back to its old pursuits in a combination of complacency and despair. As ever, the rumor mills ground on. The Americans were the arbiters of fate. There was no limit to American duplicity, the people of Saigon felt, as there was no limit to American power.

An ARVN casualty of the spring 1972 NVA invasion of South Vietnam.

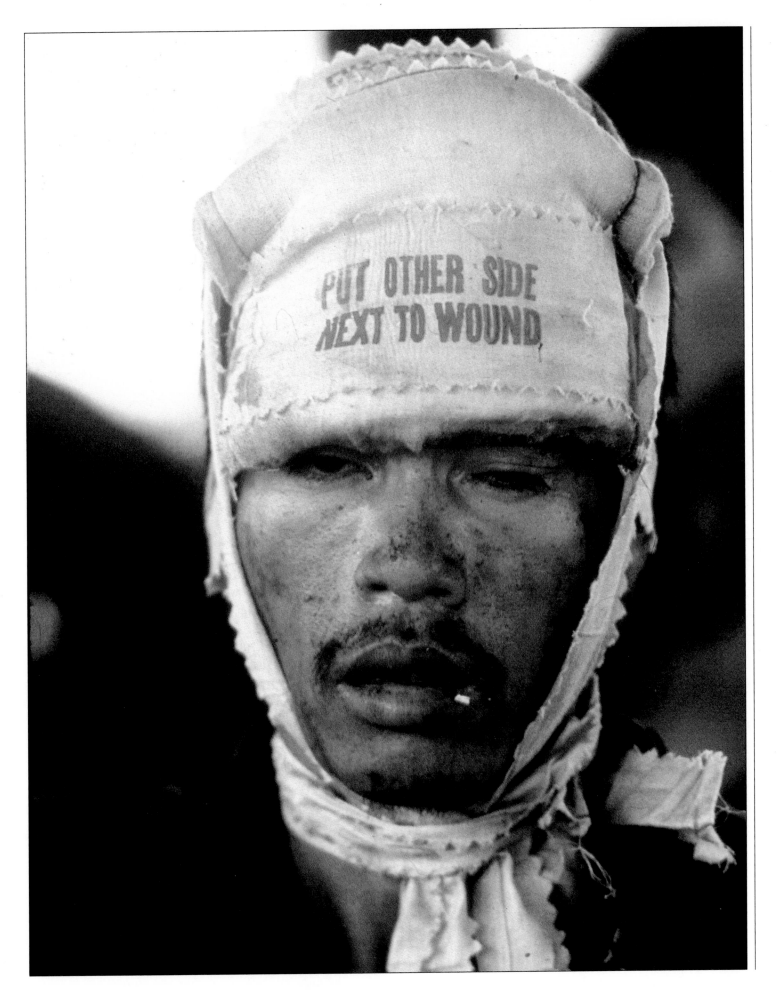

Slain ARVN soldiers lie near their foxholes along Highway 1 in Dong Ha during the North's 1972 Easter offensive. The unexpected speed and scale of the offensive proved devastating to the ARVN soldiers.

Above. An ARVN soldier charges NVA positions just south of Quang Tri in April 1972.

Right. After a skirmish north of Hue, ARVN troops huddle near the bodies of NVA soldiers.

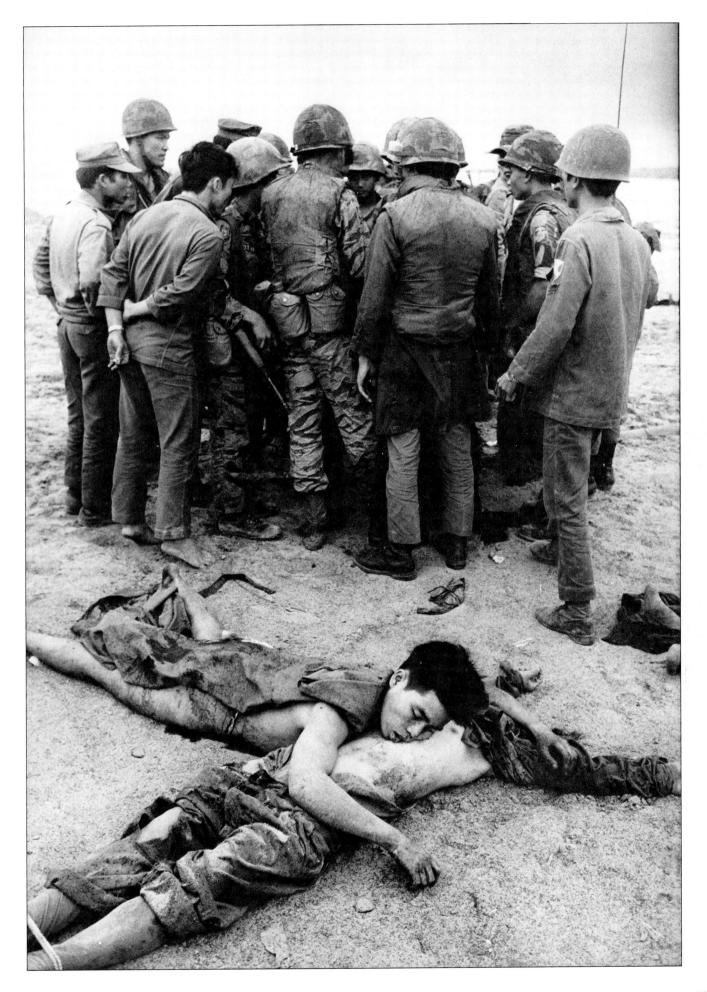

A medevac helicopter collects wounded in Quang Tri Province during the Easter offensive.

The bodies of South Vietnamese killed during the North Vietnamese offensive lie along Highway 1 between Quang Tri and Hue. Thousands of soldiers and civilians fled south to Hue, leaving behind a trail of dead as the NVA pressed the attack.

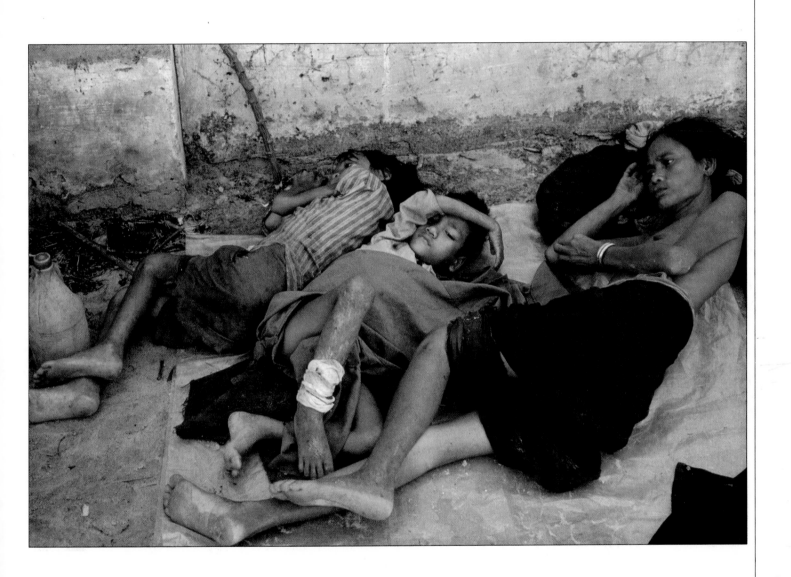

Montagnard refugees find shelter in one of
the last undestroyed buildings of An Loc,
which was besieged by the NVA for
ninety-two days. An ARVN relief column
trying to fight its way in to An Loc never
broke through, leaving U.S. air power as
the last resort for supporting the defenders
inside the city.

Above. A victorious ARVN soldier stands amid the ruins of Quang Tri after the city was retaken from the NVA by South Vietnamese forces.

Right. An Loc, the capital of Binh Duong Province, lies shattered after the Easter offensive. Weeks of North Vietnamese artillery assaults were matched by intensive U.S. bombing, leaving the city a ghostly skeleton.

The End

During the winter rains of 1975, Phuoc Binh, a provincial capital north of Saigon, fell to NVA regulars. Their heavy guns pulverized the city. Eight thousand strong, they stormed the ARVN perimeter.

Ho Chi Minh was dead, and Ngo Dinh Diem, and Vietnamese in numbers beyond estimation; nailed by the bombs, smoked by the Spooky gunships, buried by NVA 85s. They had died holding each other's hands and donkey-riding their wounded out. Or carrying their teapots—the women were always carrying teapots—and carrying their children and the children carrying children. The soil and the dead were commingled. The morning mists were filled with humble ghosts.

John Kennedy was dead. Lyndon Johnson was dead. Mac V had faded away. More than 50,000 Americans were dead and their futures lost to us.

When the dry season came, NVA Chief of Staff General Van Tien Dung felt the earth firm beneath his feet. Like many others, he would write a book about the war later on. It would be a book entitled, without irony, *Our Great Spring Victory*. In his book General Dung recalls the jungle in dry weather, the clearings "whose dry leaves covered the ground like a yellow carpet." The dry earth would be good for tanks, General Dung thought.

In Saigon, President Thieu's family was speculating in real estate. No one could believe it. Real estate was such a bad bet. There were no more American advisers and no more B-52s.

In March, General Dung's forces feinted toward Pleiku, panicked its garrison, then shifted directions to cut the highway to Ban Me Thuot. Ban Me Thuot fell on the tenth of March. President Thieu decided on a strategic withdrawal, the better to re-form and fight on a solid southern front. He ordered his commander in II Corps to evacuate Pleiku. The commanding general, overcome with terror, fled with his staff, leaving his army. And then it all fell apart.

Thieu ordered Hue held to the last man, then changed his orders and called for retreat. The troops in Hue, officials and their families and ordinary people who had learned a fear from which they would never be free, recalled the terror visited on the city during Tet, 1968. As the soldiers and their families fled Pleiku and Hue, the NVA fired shell after shell into their ranks. Hysterical thousands, crazy with fear, crazy with thirst and hunger, poured into Da Nang. Many carried dead or dying children.

What followed has often been recounted and need not be again. More horrors ensued, more, it might be thought, than such a small country could contain.

Late in April, just before the fall, President Thieu and his family left with their money. In Saigon, other families committed suicide, policemen shot themselves on street corners, Catholic soldiers emptied their rifles into each other, striving for grace. The Americans managed to get their own out, but Vietnamese who deserted the Vietcong, loyal Nungs guarding abandoned apartment houses, native CIA operatives and lists containing their names were mostly left behind for the Northern security services to deal with.

A tank pulled up in front of the presidential palace and an NVA colonel, the correspondent of the Red Army newspaper, accepted surrender from a corps of old men whose day was done.

Incredibly, there seemed to be no more Americans. We had gone home, out of their history at last, to sing our own songs and tell our own stories. The country of Vietnam fell into the hands of its inhabitants.

During the evacuation, two young U.S. Marines were killed by enemy rocket fire on the tarmac of Tan Son Nhut. They were the last known Americans killed in Vietnam.

Some called their deaths unnecessary. There had been another miscalculation up the line. Operation Talon Vise, the final extrication of the American mission, had been delayed to the point of near disaster.

But by that time fairly few Americans were in the mood for outrage or name calling or affixing blame. There had been so many miscalculations, just as there had been unheralded acts of valor that lent meaning to obscure deaths and the lives behind them. There had been so much outrage and so much suffering. It had been so bitter and so never ending. It had torn apart America and destroyed Vietnam.

Who can speak of unnecessary deaths in such a war, or in any war?

A South Vietnamese veteran leads other refugees toward the coastal city of Nha Trang after fleeing the NVA's advance into the central highlands town of Ban Me Thuot.

Northeast of Saigon, civilians fleeing the fighting at Xuan Loc prepare to board helicopters landing supplies for ARVN troops fighting one of their final stands. Despite their stiff defense, the South Vietnamese succumbed to the NVA assault of Xuan Loc, April 20.

With most of South Vietnam in Communist hands and with the fall of Saigon imminent, the Americans began the official evacuation of U.S. citizens and their employees from the embassy in Saigon. Here thousands of Vietnamese storm the embassy in a desperate attempt to leave the crumbling nation.

Above. Under Communist machine-gun fire, a South Vietnamese soldier huddles next to a wounded comrade on the Newport Bridge in Saigon on April 28, 1975. The NVA took the bridge, closing off the last major highway leading into the capital.

Refugees arriving at Nha Trang on April 1 in overloaded barges discover a shocking sight on the wharf: the bodies of dozens of other refugees, trampled to death by South Vietnamese soldiers and others fleeing the Communist advance. The barges docked, took on fresh water, then headed for Saigon.

Left above. One of the last to leave the embassy, U.S. Ambassador Graham Martin disembarks from an evacuation helicopter on the deck of the U.S.S. Blue Ridge *on April 30, 1975.*

Left below. On April 21, 1975, declaring that "The United States had not respected its promises," President Nguyen Van Thieu of South Vietnam resigns.

Above. During the American evacuation of Saigon, an Air America crewman helps evacuees into a helicopter perched atop an apartment building. The evacuation plans nearly dissolved in chaos when thousands of refugees attempted to flee the city.

The South falls. A Communist tank flying the NLF flag crashes through the gates of the presidential palace in Saigon on April 30, 1975. Several hours before, acting South Vietnamese leader Duong Van Minh had announced the unconditional surrender of South Vietnam.

Epilogue

When lilacs last in the dooryard
    bloom'd
And the great star early droop'd in the
    western sky in the night,
I mourn'd—and yet shall mourn with
    ever-returning spring.
             —Walt Whitman

*Right. Combat veteran Earl Robinson
watches the Armed Forces Day Parade in
Chattanooga, Tennessee, May 15, 1976.*

*Following pages. The Vietnam Veterans
Memorial in Washington, D.C.*

Picture Credits

Cover Photograph:
Catherine Leroy

Introduction
p. 6, left, UPI/Bettmann Newsphotos; right, Don McCullin—Magnum. p. 7, top left, UPI/Bettmann Newsphotos; bottom left, Eddie Adams—AP/Wide World. pp. 7, right, 8, left, Larry Burrows—LIFE Magazine, © 1966, Time Inc. p. 8, top right, UPI/Bettmann Newsphotos; bottom right, John Filo, courtesy Valley News Dispatch. p. 9, left, Larry Burrows—LIFE Magazine, © 1966, Time Inc.; right, AP/Wide World.

Resisting the French
p. 13, Johnny Florea—LIFE Magazine, © 1945, Time Inc. p. 14, Ngo Vinh Long Collection. p. 16, top, Camera Press Ltd.; bottom, Archimedes L. A. Patti Collection. p. 17, Vietnam News Agency. p. 18, Ngo Vinh Long Collection. pp. 20-21, Howard Sochurek—LIFE Magazine, © 1951, Time Inc. p. 22, E. C. P. Armées. p. 24, Daniel Camus—Service Press Information, courtesy LIFE Magazine. p. 25, Nihon Denpa News, Ltd. p. 26, Daniel Camus—Paris Match. p. 27, Howard Sochurek—LIFE Magazine, © 1960, Time Inc.

Saigon
p. 29, Bruno Barbey—Magnum. p. 30, Howard Sochurek—LIFE Magazine, © 1955, Time Inc. p. 31, Malcolm Browne—AP/Wide World. p. 32, © Julian Wasser. p. 33, Harry Redl. p. 34, Angelo Cozzi, Milan. p. 36, Y. R. Okamoto, courtesy LBJ Library. p. 37, Ray Cranbourne—Black Star. p. 38, Dick Swanson—Black Star. p. 39, Larry Burrows—LIFE Magazine, © 1969, Time Inc. p. 40, James H. Pickerell—Black Star. pp. 41-42, James H. Karales. p. 43, Philip Jones Griffiths—Magnum. p. 44, Agence France Presse.

War in the Village
p. 47, Philip Jones Griffiths—Magnum. p. 48, Larry Burrows—LIFE Magazine, © 1972, Time Inc. p. 49, Armand Latourre—Camera Press Ltd. p. 50, Roger Pic. p. 52, Hilmar Pabel, Rimsting/Chiemsee. p. 53, Philip Jones Griffiths—Magnum. p. 54, Bruno Barbey—Magnum. p. 56, © Larry Burrows Collection. p. 57, Paul Schutzer—LIFE Magazine, © 1965, Time Inc. p. 58, Dana Stone—Black Star. p. 60, Philip Jones Griffiths—Magnum. p. 61, Goro Nakamura.

Strategy of Attrition
p. 63, Don McCullin—Camera Press Ltd. pp. 64-65, Larry Burrows—LIFE Magazine, © 1963, Time Inc. p. 66, © Larry Burrows Collection. pp. 68-69, Larry Burrows—LIFE Magazine, © 1966, Time Inc. p. 70, Paul Schutzer—LIFE Magazine, © 1965, Time Inc. pp. 71-72, Philip Jones Griffiths—Magnum. p. 74, Larry Burrows—LIFE Magazine, © 1966, Time Inc. p. 75, Frank Johnston—UPI/

Bettmann Newsphotos. pp. 76-77, Catherine Leroy. p. 78, Co Rentmeester—LIFE Magazine, © 1967, Time Inc.

The Other Side
p. 81, J. P. Moscardo—Agence ANA. p. 82, Roger Pic. p. 84, Marc Riboud. p. 85, Marc Riboud—Magnum. p. 86, Vietnam News Agency. pp. 88-89, Nihon Denpa News, Ltd. p. 90, Marc Riboud. p. 92, Thomas Billhardt, Berlin, GDR. p. 93, left, Roger Pic; right, SYGMA. p. 94, Vietnam News Agency.

Khe Sanh
pp. 97-106, David Douglas Duncan.

Tet!
p. 109, Don McCullin—Magnum. p. 110, AP/Wide World. p. 112, Don McCullin—Magnum. p. 113, Philip Jones Griffiths—Magnum. p. 114, John Olson—TIME MAGAZINE. p. 115, Philip Jones Griffiths—Magnum. pp. 116-17, Don McCullin—Magnum. p. 118, Catherine Leroy/Gamma-Liaison. p. 119, Don McCullin—Magnum. pp. 120-21, Ghislain Bellorget. p. 122, Larry Burrows—LIFE Magazine, © 1969, Time Inc. p. 123, Don McCullin—Magnum.

War at Home
p. 125, Paul Schutzer—LIFE Magazine, © 1960, Time Inc. p. 126, Charles Harbutt—Archive. p. 128, Bernard Boston. p. 129, Charles Gatewood. p. 130, Moneta Sleet, Jr.—AP/Wide World. p. 131, Bill Eppridge—LIFE Magazine, © 1968, Time Inc. p. 132, Ray Mews—AP/Wide World. p. 133, Jack Kightlinger, courtesy LBJ Library. p. 134, Burt Glinn—Magnum. p. 135, Perry C. Riddle. p. 136, Jeffrey Blankfort—Jeroboam. p. 138, Michael Abramson/Gamma-Liaison. p. 139, Stephen Shames—Visions. p. 140, George Butler. p. 142, Charles Gatewood—Magnum. p. 143, Ollie Atkins—Nixon Project/National Archives. p. 144, Bill Ray—LIFE Magazine, © 1966, Time Inc. p. 145, Bernard Edelman.

Withdrawal
p. 147, John Robaton. p. 148, Dirck Halstead—UPI/Bettmann Newsphotos. p. 149, © Al Rockoff. p. 150, © David Burnett 1983—Contact. p. 151, Mark Jury. p. 153, Philip Jones Griffiths—Magnum. p. 154, Larry Burrows—LIFE Magazine, © 1972, Time Inc. p. 155, Larry Burrows—LIFE Magazine, © 1970, Time Inc. pp. 156-57, Mark Jury. p. 158, Akihiko Okamura. p. 160, Angelo Cozzi, Milan. p. 161, Ian Berry—Magnum. p. 162, Michel Laurent/Gamma-Liaison. p. 163, Roger Pic/Gamma-Liaison.

The Easter Offensive
pp. 165-66, Don McCullin—The Sunday Times, London. pp. 168-69, © David Burnett 1983—Contact. pp. 170-72, Don McCullin—The Sunday Times, London. pp. 173-74, Bruno Barbey—Magnum. p. 175, © David Burnett 1984—Contact.

The End
p. 177, AP/Wide World. p. 178, Hiroji Kubota—Magnum. p. 180, Nik Wheeler—Black Star. p. 181, Phuc—UPI/Bettmann Newsphotos. p. 182, Jean-Claude Françolon/Gamma-Liaison. p. 184, top, UPI/Bettmann Newsphotos; bottom, Dirck Halstead/Gamma-Liaison. p. 185, UPI/Bettmann Newsphotos. p. 186, Françoise Demulder/Gamma-Liaison.

Epilogue
p. 189, Robin Hood. p. 190, © 1984 Everett C. Johnson—Folio.